Advance Praise for *Getting Teacher Evaluation Right*

"This book is a must-read for anyone who wants to improve teaching and learning, rather than simply wax poetic about it. Darling-Hammond has given us a practical roadmap to success based on research and best practice. To do teacher evaluation right, we must build a system designed to support teaching that is based on rigorous standards, analyzing student work from multiple sources, and continuous feedback focused on improvement and embedded in teacher collaboration."

—**Randi Weingarten**, President,
American Federation of Teachers

"With all the interest, growing confusion, and outright wrong steps applied to teacher evaluation, there could not be a more needed and timely contribution than Linda Darling-Hammond's *Getting Teacher Evaluation Right*. This is a systemic, clear, inspiring, and actionable framework for developing the teaching profession."

—**Michael Fullan**, Professor Emeritus,
OISE/University of Toronto

"If anybody knows how to get teacher evaluation right, it is Linda Darling-Hammond. Her new book presents a system that includes development and support, in addition to teacher assessment, and promotes teaching as a collegial activity, rather than reinforcing isolation and competitiveness."

—**Dan Domenech**, Executive Director,
American Association of School Administrators

"Why and how to evaluate teachers in our public schools have become common themes in global education reforms. This book is a myth-breaker and a must-read for anybody who wishes to understand the complexity of teacher quality and evaluation."

—**Pasi Sahlberg**, Director General of CIMO, Helsinki,
author of award-winning book, *Finnish Lessons* (2011)

"Finally, a book that captures what educators have been saying. This is a must-read for those interested in building a world-class education system!"

—**Dennis Van Roekel**, National Education Association

"This stimulating and provocative book outlines a comprehensive system for the development, support, and assessment of teaching. This is a must-read for educational leaders and policymakers at all levels who should pay heed to Darling-Hammond's sensible, practical plan of action for *Getting Teacher Evaluation Right.*"

—**Gail Connelly**, Executive Director,
National Association of Elementary School Principals

"Darling-Hammond knows that we must 'get teacher evaluation right' and her book is as clear a guide for doing that as we will ever see."

—**Ronald Thorpe**,
National Board for Professional Teaching Standards

"In *Getting Teacher Evaluation Right,* Darling-Hammond emphasizes elements essential to creating an evaluation system that contributes to better student outcomes, including the role of continuous support for teachers and the profession, and the collective aspects of improving teaching. This book offers well-conceived guidance to address a complex and thorny topic."

—**Stephanie Hirsh**, Executive Director, Learning Forward

"Regardless of where one currently stands on teacher evaluation issues, a trusted, well-researched, comprehensive framework is needed to help navigate the complex policy issues facing policymakers at the local, state, and national levels. This book provides that framework and much more."

—**Jim Kohlmoos**, Former Executive Director,
National Association of State Boards of Education

Getting Teacher Evaluation Right

What Really Matters for Effectiveness and Improvement

Linda Darling-Hammond

Teachers College, Columbia University
New York and London

Oxford, OH
www.learningforward.org

Published simultaneously by Teachers College Press, 1234 Amsterdam Avenue, New York, NY 10027 and Learning Forward, 504 S. Locust Street, Oxford, OH 45056

The following source is quoted in Chapters 2 and 6: *Professional learning in the learning profession: A status report on teacher development in the United States and abroad,* by National Staff Development Council, *Report,* February 2009. Reprinted with permission of Learning Forward, www.learingforward.org. All rights reserved.

Library of Congress Cataloging-in-Publication Data

Darling-Hammond, Linda, 1951–
   Getting teacher evaluation right : what really matters for effectiveness and improvement / Linda Darling-Hammond.
     pages cm
   Includes bibliographical references and index.
   ISBN 978-0-8077-5446-7 (pbk. : alk. paper)—ISBN 978-0-8077-5447-4 (hardcover : alk. paper)
    1. Teachers—Rating of—United States.   2. Teaching—United States—Evaluation.   I. Title.
LB2838.D28 2013
371.14'4—dc23   2013001075

ISBN 978-0-8077-5446-7 (paper)
ISBN 978-0-8077-5447-4 (hardcover)

Printed on acid-free paper
Manufactured in the United States of America

20   19   18   17   16   15   14   13   8   7   6   5   4   3   2   1

Contents

Preface

I wrote this book in response to requests for help from teachers, principals, superintendents, school board members, and state officials who are trying to sort out the current maelstrom of ideas about teacher evaluation that have swept the country. Prodded by the requirements of Race to the Top grants and federal waivers from No Child Left Behind, states and districts across the United States have been changing their policies at a dizzying rate, often with little chance to consider the research base for practice. Most are trying to accommodate these new mandates while constructing productive, manageable systems that support high-quality practice, teacher learning, and student success.

This is no easy feat. There are many landmines in this territory, and little available information that can offer decision makers both research evidence and practical examples to inform this work. This book was written to address this need. It is intended to help state and local policymakers and practitioners imagine and create coherent systems for evaluating teachers in ways that support continuous improvement in classrooms and schools.

I argue in this book that we should think about teacher evaluation as part of a teaching and learning *system* that creates a set of coherent, well-grounded supports for strong teaching throughout the profession. In addition to clear standards for student learning, accompanied by high-quality curriculum materials and assessments, this system should include five key elements:

1. **Common statewide standards** for teaching that are related to meaningful student learning and are shared across the profession;
2. **Performance-based assessments, based on these standards, guiding state functions,** such as teacher preparation, licensure, and advanced certification;

3. **Local evaluation systems aligned to the same standards,** for evaluating on-the-job teaching based on multiple measures of teaching practice and student learning;
4. **Aligned professional learning opportunities** that support the improvement of teachers and teaching quality; and
5. **Support structures** to ensure properly trained evaluators, mentoring for teachers who need additional assistance, and fair and timely decisions about personnel actions.

The book is organized to illustrate how each of these five elements should operate within a system that supports effective teaching and learning, based on evidence from research and best practice in the field. Following the initial chapter, which describes this approach, I take up, in Chapter 2, the issue of standards for learning aligned with standards for teaching: the initial stepping stones for a comprehensive system. I describe how these teaching standards should guide assessments throughout the entire career: from preservice through initial licensure, induction, professional licensure, and recognition of accomplished practice.

In Chapter 3, I describe what states could do, based on these standards, to create an aligned system of performance assessments for evaluating teaching from preparation and licensing through induction, to advanced certification. In Chapter 4, I show how local districts can create complementary systems of local evaluation, based on the same standards, that support assessment and ongoing development, enabling growth over the course of the teaching career. I describe some of the many productive ways to build a standards-based system that incorporates evidence of practice, student learning, and professional contributions.

However, we have also discovered potential pitfalls of efforts to tie student achievement to teacher evaluation in inappropriate ways. I discuss these in Chapter 5, along with more useful strategies for connecting teaching, learning, and evaluation. Because student learning is the primary goal of teaching, it appears straightforward that it ought to be taken into account in determining a teacher's competence. Yet how to do so is not so simple. As I describe in this chapter, the currently touted strategy of using value-added methods to calculate student test score gains attached to individual teachers has been found to be far less reliable and accurate than many researchers had hoped and most policymakers have assumed. Other strategies that use multiple sources of evidence about student learning are essential to get a fair gauge on what a teacher has accomplished with his or her students. I document some of the work of schools and districts that have figured out how to do this well.

One critically important feature of productive strategies is that they require teachers to collect, examine, interpret, and use evidence about student learning to reflect on and plan instruction, and to inform improvements. Equally important are the incentives and opportunities for ongoing professional learning that give teachers the knowledge and skills that allow them to respond to evidence of student learning in ever-more-effective ways. I turn to this issue in Chapter 6. As the examples I offer show, when schools learn to create better conditions for teaching and learning, individual and collective teaching practice can improve.

Having good ideas about how to measure teaching is not enough to have a good evaluation system. One serious shortcoming of teacher evaluation reforms is that they have often focused on designing instruments for observing teachers, without developing the structural elements of a sound evaluation system. In Chapter 7 I discuss these elements, which include trained, skilled evaluators; supports for teachers needing assistance; governance structures that enable sound personnel decisions; and resources to sustain the system.

Finally, systems should be designed to be manageable and feasible, not so complex that they overwhelm the participants with requirements and paperwork. In Chapter 8, I discuss how to accomplish this with the necessary systems and supports that allow educators to focus productively on improving teaching. I hope this book helps all the members of the education community design teacher evaluation that works to achieve its most important goals: more responsive and effective teaching in each and every classroom and across the system as a whole.

—Linda Darling-Hammond
Stanford University
March 19, 2013

Acknowledgments

There are always many people to appreciate for any significant piece of work, and this is no exception. Before I thank those who helped to create this book, however, my first thanks go to U.S. public school teachers, who work harder and accomplish more than most people in any line of work in any country in the world. This book is written to support your efforts, and to strengthen your ability to reach each of your students in all the ways that you strive to do.

I am especially grateful for the expert assistance of Channa Mae Cook, who conducted interviews, observations, and background research for this study, and to Ann Jaquith and Madlene Hamilton, who also conducted background research on specific program models. I thank Sonya Keller, who ably supported the process of finalizing the manuscript and securing permissions.

The original inspiration for this book was the Good Schools Seminar Series, supported by the Albert Shanker Institute, a non-profit, nonpartisan organization endowed by the American Federation of Teachers to promote excellence in public education. The Good Schools Seminar is an effort to build a network of union leaders, district superintendents, and researchers to work collaboratively on improving public education through a focus on teaching.

Many wise educators contributed to this discussion: Barbara Byrd Bennett, now Chief Academic Officer for Chicago Public Schools; Larry Carter, Jr., President, United Teachers of New Orleans; Leo Casey, then Vice President for Academic High Schools, United Federation of Teachers; Tom Forkner, President, Anderson Federation of Teachers; Dal Lawrence, former President, Toledo Federation of Teachers; Francine Lawrence, Executive Vice President, American Federation of Teachers; Daniel J. Montgomery, President and Chief Operating Officer, Illinois Federation of Teachers; Jody

Papini, Douglas County Federation of Teachers; Mary Cathryn Ricker, President, St. Paul Federation of Teachers; Mary Ronan, Superintendent, Cincinnati Public Schools; Nathan Saunders, President, Washington Teachers Unions; Julie Sellers, Cincinnati Federation of Teachers; Rod Sherman, President, Plattsburgh Teachers Association; Brenda Smith, President, Douglas County Federation of Teachers; and Zelda Smith, New Orleans Public Schools. Eugenia Kemble, executive director of the Shanker Institute, and Joan Baratz Snowden, consultant to the American Federation of Teachers, also offered helpful comments on the document.

Adriane Dorrington, Senior Policy Analyst, and Bill Raabe, Director of the Center for Great Public Schools, supported my efforts to identify districts with productive evaluation practices. I have also learned from my collaboration with the Accomplished California Teachers (ACT) network, a project of the National Board Resource Center at Stanford University, which has convened a remarkable group of expert teachers to deliberate and advise on critical policy issues in teaching, including teacher evaluation. The ACT report, *A Quality Teacher in Every Classroom*, has informed my thinking and this book. Special thanks go to ACT director and associate director Sandy Dean and David Cohen, respectively, as well as the talented teachers who are part of ACT, for their tireless efforts on behalf of teaching, learning, and children in California.

In addition, I am grateful for useful feedback and advice from Barnett Berry, President of the Center for Teaching Quality; Gail Connelly, Executive Director of the National Association of Elementary School Principals; Dan Domenech, Executive Director of the American Association of School Administrators; Rebecca Pringle, Secretary-Treasurer of the National Education Association; Jim Kohlmoos, Executive Director of the National Association of State Boards of Education (NASBE), and NASBE staff members Liz Ross and Patty Yoo; Janice Poda, Education Workforce Strategic Initiative Director, and Kathleen Paliokas, InTASC Program Director, at the Council for Chief State School Officers; Adam Urbanski, Director of the Teacher Union Reform Network; and Arthur Wise, President Emeritus of the National Council for Accreditation of Teacher Education.

Support for this work was provided by the Ford Foundation and the Sandler Foundation through grants to the Stanford Center for Opportunity Policy in Education (SCOPE), which published a shorter monograph on this topic. We are grateful for their investment in this work.

Think Systemically

I have had administrators who never came into my classroom for formal observations or asked me for anything more than the initial planning/goal sheet. I have had administrators observe a formal lesson and put the feedback sheet in my box without ever having spoken to me about the lesson, and I have had years where I am just asked to sign the end-of-the year evaluation sheet [without being observed].

—*Jane Fung, National Board Certified teacher and Milken Award Winner,[1] California*

The United States is at a critical moment in teacher evaluation. The evaluation process is undergoing extensive changes, some of them quite radical, in nearly every state and district across the country. As states and districts embark on these reforms, it is crucial for schools, teachers, and especially students that we move practice forward to improve the quality of teaching while avoiding potential pitfalls that could damage education. It is imperative that we not substitute new problems for familiar ones, but that we instead use this moment of transformation to get teacher evaluation right.

Virtually everyone agrees that teacher evaluation in the United States needs an overhaul. Existing systems rarely help teachers improve or clearly distinguish those who are succeeding from those who are struggling. The tools that are used do not always represent the important features of good teaching. It is nearly impossible for principals, especially in large schools, to have sufficient time or content expertise to evaluate all of the teachers they supervise, much less to address the needs of some teachers for intense instructional support. And many principals have not had access to the professional development and support they need to become expert instructional leaders and evaluators of teaching. Thus, evaluation in its current form often contributes little either to teacher learning or to accurate, timely information for personnel decisions.

These problems are long-standing. They were obvious when my colleagues and I first studied teacher evaluation systems in the United States in the early 1980s.[2] As part of a RAND Corporation study, Arthur Wise, Milbrey McLaughlin, Harriet Bernstein, and I searched the country for effective evaluation systems and found the process rather like rummaging for the proverbial needle in a haystack. We discovered only a very few that offered opportunities for teachers to set goals and receive regular, useful feedback, along with systems that could support both learning and timely, effective personnel decisions.

There were some bright spots, like the then-brand-new Toledo Peer Assessment and Review model—a labor-management breakthrough that introduced intensive mentoring and peer evaluation for both novice teachers and struggling veterans, and that ensured serious decisions for tenure and continuation. Also noteworthy was the Greenwich, Connecticut, model of teacher goal-setting and continuous feedback—which involved teachers in collecting evidence about their practice and student learning long before this was fashionable elsewhere. Although the use of some of these successful models has spread, the broad landscape for teacher evaluation has changed little, and impatience with the results of weak systems has grown.

Today, teacher evaluation is receiving unprecedented attention, in large part because new teacher evaluation systems are a requirement for states and districts that want to receive funding under the federal "Race to the Top" initiative or flexibility waivers under the No Child Left Behind Act. As teaching has become a major focus of policy attention, teacher evaluation is currently the primary tool being promoted to improve it. Federal requirements include the use of multiple categories of teacher ratings, rather than just "satisfactory" or "unsatisfactory," based on multiple observations, feedback, and the use of student test scores to assess effectiveness. They also encourage the use of these evaluations to inform decisions about tenure and continuation, compensation, promotion, advanced certification, and dismissal. As a consequence, most states in the country are in the process of dramatically overhauling their evaluation systems for both teachers and administrators.

Although there is widespread consensus that teacher evaluation in the United States needs serious attention, it is important to recognize that changing on-the-job evaluation will not, by itself, transform the quality of teaching. For all of the attention focused on identifying and removing poor teachers, we will not really improve the quality of the profession if we do not also cultivate an excellent supply of good teachers who are well prepared and committed to career-long learning. And teachers' ongoing learning, in turn, depends on the construction of a strong professional development system and useful career development approaches that can help spread expertise. Finally, improving the skills of individual teachers will not be enough: We need to create and sustain productive, collegial working conditions that allow teachers to work collectively in an environment that supports learning for them and their students.

In short, what we really need in the United States is a conception of teacher evaluation as part of a *teaching and learning system* that supports continuous improvement, both for individual teachers and for the profession as a whole. Such a system should enhance teacher learning and skill, while at the same time ensuring that teachers who are retained and tenured can effectively support student learning throughout their careers.

This book seeks to outline how such a comprehensive system for the development, support, and assessment of teaching would operate if it were based on research and best practices currently found in the field. It also describes where reforms of teacher evaluation can go awry, by creating unmanageable systems, using tools that are not reliable measures of teacher effectiveness, or reinforcing isolation and competitiveness rather than joint work among teachers. Finally, it examines how the contexts for teaching must evolve so that teaching is supported as the collegial activity it must be to promote student learning.

Of all lessons for teacher evaluation in the current era, perhaps this one is the most important: that we not adopt an individualistic, competitive approach to ranking and sorting teachers that undermines the growth of learning communities which will, at the end of the day, do more to support student achievement than dozens of the most elaborate ranking schemes ever could.

> **The growth of learning communities will do more to support student achievement than dozens of the most elaborate (teacher) ranking schemes ever could.**

Before we can build these more productive systems, however, we need to understand where most current schools are struggling and why. Understanding the source of the problems is key to finding the right solutions.

PROBLEMS WITH CURRENT EVALUATION SYSTEMS

In a recent report on teacher evaluation,[3] a group of expert teachers—the Accomplished California Teachers (ACT) network—identified these problems with many of the district evaluation procedures they had experienced:

- **Lack of consistent, clear standards of good practice**: The standards statements that attempt to guide teaching practice often list the elements of effective teaching but fail to elaborate what constitutes evidence of these, thus hampering accurate, fair, and reliable assessment of a teacher's work, and clarity about how to improve.
- **No focus on improving practice**: Discussion about ways to improve the quality of the teaching performance is very often left out of the follow-up conversation, if there is one.
- **Inadequate time and staff for effective evaluations**: In many schools, especially large ones and under-resourced schools serving high-needs populations, principals have little time or training for evaluation, and even less for teacher support.
- **Little or no consideration of student outcomes**: Most evaluations pay little or no attention to the performance of a teacher's students, and hence provide little advice about

how to support student learning. The ACT teachers noted: "As long as the class is well managed and *seems* to be on task, not much else matters."

- **Cookie-cutter procedures that don't consider teacher needs**: Evaluation procedures are typically determined by contract rules and seniority (with greater frequency for novices) rather than by teacher needs. There is little consideration of which teachers could benefit from being evaluated, how often, in what manner, and by whom.
- **Detachment of evaluations from professional development**: Evaluation is rarely used to help teachers access professional development to address their unique learning needs.

These teachers are not alone. In a survey of 1,010 teachers across the nation, researchers found that:

> Teachers indicate that the most obvious technique used to assess teacher quality—the formal observation and evaluation—is not doing the job. In fact, only 26% of teachers report that their own most recent formal evaluation was "useful and effective." The plurality—41%—say it was "just a formality," while another 32% say at best it was "well-intentioned but not particularly helpful" to their teaching practice. Almost 7 in 10 teachers (69%) say that when they hear a teacher at their school has been awarded tenure, they think that it's "just a formality—it has very little to do with whether a teacher is good or not."[1]

In addition to the problems just noted, criteria and methods for evaluating teachers vary substantially across schools and districts, and these are typically disconnected from the ways teachers are evaluated at key career milestones—when they complete preservice teacher education, when they become initially licensed, and when they are tenured and receive a longer-term professional license. As a consequence, over the course of their careers, most teachers experience a cacophony of standards and directives—both in terms of *what* they are expected to teach and *how* they are expected to do so. In short, many states have no coherent system for evaluating and improving teaching, which makes it difficult to come up with effective solutions to the problems of teaching practice we face. The ACT report observes:

> The links between existing policies for preparation, induction, ongoing evaluation, and professional development are weak or non-existent now, and the result is a patchwork of programs that don't achieve the purpose of creating a system that ensures and promotes quality teaching at all levels of teacher development.[5]

As my colleagues and I found in our research nearly 30 years ago, and as I experienced as a high school teacher some years ago myself, most teachers want more from an evaluation system. They crave useful feedback and the challenge and counsel that would enable them to improve. Far from ducking the issue of evaluation, they want more robust systems that are useful, fair, and pointed at productive development. The ACT teachers noted:

> We worry that the future of our young colleagues in teaching may not fulfill the promise we have dreamed of for our profession, where the highest consideration is given to teachers' important questions: "How am I doing?" and "What can I do better?" We want evaluation that offers answers to those questions, that paints a detailed picture of good teaching, that serves to guide professional development, and that lays out a clear, coherent path through a teacher's career where the expectation is for continual improvement.[6]

HOW SHOULD WE THINK ABOUT THE IMPROVEMENT OF TEACHING?

Some proponents of teacher evaluation reforms have conjectured that if districts would eliminate the bottom 5 to 10% of teachers each year, as measured by value-added student test scores, U.S. student achievement would increase by a substantial amount—enough to catch up to high-achieving countries like Finland.[7] However, there is no real-world evidence to support this idea and quite a bit to dispute it. (I discuss this evidence in later chapters.)

In fact, high-achieving Finland does not do what these advocates propose. Rather than focusing on firing teachers, it has one of the strongest initial teacher education systems in the world, and leaders credit that system with having produced nationwide improvements in student learning.[8] (See box: How Finland Develops Effective Teachers.) There is relatively little emphasis in Finland on formal on-the-job evaluation, and much more emphasis on collaboration among professionals to promote student learning. In truth, we cannot fire our way to Finland. If we want to reach the high and equitable outcomes it has achieved in recent years, we will have to *teach* our way to stronger student learning by supporting teachers' collective learning.

Despite the current focus on inservice evaluation, a highly skilled teaching force results from developing well-prepared teachers from recruitment through preparation through ongoing professional development. Support for teacher learning and evaluation needs to be part of an integrated whole that promotes effectiveness during every stage of a teacher's career. Such a system must ensure that teacher evaluation is connected to—not isolated from— preparation and induction programs, daily professional practice, and a productive instructional context.

> **A system must ensure that teacher evaluation is connected to—not isolated from—preparation and induction, daily practice, and a productive instructional context.**

At the center of such a system are professional teaching standards that are linked to student learning standards, curriculum, and assessment, thereby creating a seamless relationship between what teachers do in the classroom and how they are prepared and assessed. A productive evaluation system should consider teachers' practice in the context of curriculum goals and students' needs, as well as multifaceted evidence of teachers' contributions to student learning and to the school as a whole. And it should create the structures that make good evaluation possible: time and training for evaluators, the support of master or mentor teachers to provide needed expertise and assistance, and high-quality, accessible learning opportunities supporting effectiveness for all teachers at every stage of their careers.

If learning to teach is to be a cumulative, coherent experience, a common framework should guide a comprehensive system that addresses a variety of purposes:

- initial and continuing teacher licensing,
- hiring and early induction,
- granting tenure,
- support for supervision and professional learning,
- identification of teachers who need additional assistance, and
- recognition of expert teachers who can contribute to the learning of their peers, both informally and as mentors, coaches, and teacher leaders.

The system must also allow for the fair and timely removal of teachers who do not improve with feedback and assistance. It may also be asked to support decisions about compensation, as policymakers are increasingly interested in tying compensation to judgments about teacher effectiveness, either by differentiating wages or by linking such judgments to specific responsibilities and salary increments for more expert teachers. As I discuss in Chapter 6, an approach that supports the development and sharing of greater expertise, rather than one that fosters competition and isolation, holds the most promise for improving teaching and learning overall.

> **The system must allow for the fair and timely removal of teachers who do not improve with feedback and assistance.**

HOW FINLAND DEVELOPS EFFECTIVE TEACHERS

Finland has been frequently cited as an exemplar of school improvement since it rapidly climbed to the top of the international rankings after it emerged from the Soviet Union's shadow. Once poorly ranked educationally, with a turgid bureaucratic system that produced large inequalities, it now ranks at the top of nations in the Organization for Economic Cooperation and Development (OECD) on the PISA assessments in mathematics, science, and reading. Furthermore, it has highly equitable student outcomes, even for its growing population of immigrant students from northern Africa, the Middle East, and Eastern Europe.

Finnish officials credit these gains to teacher education reforms that began in the 1970s when teacher education became a 5-year university-based program. During the 1990s, another reform of preparation increased the focus on teaching diverse learners higher-order skills such as problem solving and critical thinking in research-based master's degree programs.

Prospective teachers are competitively selected from the pool of college graduates—only 15% of those who apply are admitted—and receive a 2- to 3-year graduate-level teacher preparation program, entirely free of charge and with a living stipend. Unlike the United States, where teachers must go into debt to prepare for a profession that will pay them poorly, Finland recruits top candidates and pays them to go to school. Selection is based on academic ability, evidence of commitment to and a disposition for teaching, and capacity to read, understand, and interpret educational research. (Responding to questions about research articles is part of the admissions process.) Teaching slots are highly coveted and teacher shortages are virtually unheard of.

Teachers' preparation includes both extensive coursework on how to teach—with a strong emphasis on using state-of-the-art practice based on research—and a year of clinical experience in a model school associated with the university. These schools are intended to develop and model innovative practices, as well as to foster research on learning and teaching. Teachers are trained in research methods so that they can "contribute to an increase of the problem solving capacity of the education system,"[9] and each candidate conducts research on a problem of teaching practice as the basis for his or her master's thesis for graduation.

Within their training schools, student teachers participate in problem-solving groups, a common feature in Finnish schools. The problem-solving groups engage in a cycle of planning, action, and reflection/evaluation, which is, in fact, a model for what teachers will facilitate with their own students, who are expected to engage in a similar kind of inquiry in their studies. Indeed, the entire system is intended to improve through continual reflection,

(Continued)

evaluation, and problem solving, at the level of the classroom, school, municipality, and nation.

Teachers learn how to create challenging curriculum and how to develop performance assessments that engage students in research and inquiry. Teacher training emphasizes learning how to teach students who learn in different ways, including those with special needs. It includes a strong emphasis on "multiculturality" and the prevention of learning difficulties, as well as on the understanding of learning, thoughtful assessment, and curriculum development.[10] The egalitarian Finns reasoned that if teachers learn to help students who struggle, they will be able to teach all students more effectively and will, indeed, leave no child behind.

Most teachers now hold master's degrees in both their content area and in education, and they are well prepared to teach diverse learners—including special needs students—to foster deep understanding and to use formative performance assessments on a regular basis to inform their teaching so it meets students' needs. Teachers are well trained both in research methods and in pedagogical practice. Consequently, they are sophisticated diagnosticians, and they work together to design instruction around the national curriculum that meets the demands of the subject matter as well as the needs of their students.[11]

UNDERSTANDING *TEACHER* QUALITY
AND *TEACHING* QUALITY

In building a system, it is important not only to develop skills on the part of individual practitioners, but also to create the conditions under which practitioners can use their skills appropriately. The importance of this is easily seen if we think of medicine, where both the professional skills and professional contexts are relatively well developed through licensing of doctors and accreditation rules for hospitals, the places many physicians practice.

It would do little good to prepare doctors through intensive residencies in their specialty areas if pediatricians could be assigned to cardiac surgery or ophthalmologists were asked to treat spinal injuries. If out-of-field assignment were allowed (as it too often is in teaching), the quality of medical care would suffer even if individual doctors were highly skilled in their fields. Similarly, a cardiologist supported by the latest technology and medical resources is clearly more effective than one who has no access to heart monitors, surgical equipment, defibrillators, or medication. The quality of care is determined equally by the skill of physicians and the resources that are available to them to do their jobs.

Similarly, if one wants to ensure high-quality instruction, it is important to attend to both *teacher* quality and *teaching* quality. *Teacher quality* might be thought of as the bundle of personal traits, skills, and understandings an individual brings to teaching, including dispositions to behave in certain ways. Research on teacher effectiveness, based on teacher ratings and student achievement gains, has found the following qualities to be important:

- strong content knowledge related to what is to be taught;
- knowledge of how to teach others in that area (content pedagogy) and skill in implementing productive teaching practices;
- understanding of learners and their development, including how to support students who have learning differences or difficulties, and how to support the learning of language and content for those who are not already proficient in the language of instruction;
- general abilities to organize and explain ideas, as well as to observe and think diagnostically; and
- adaptive expertise that allows teachers to make judgments about what is likely to work in a given context in response to students' needs.[12]

Most educators, parents, and policymakers would also include important dispositions in this list, such as the willingness to:

- support learning for all students,
- teach in a fair and unbiased manner,
- adapt instruction to help students succeed,
- strive to continue to learn and improve, and
- collaborate with other professionals and parents in the service of individual students and the school as a whole.

These qualities, evidenced in research on teaching, are embodied in the standards adopted by the National Board for Professional Teaching Standards for defining accomplished teaching and, at the beginning-teacher level, by the states involved in the Interstate New Teacher Assessment and Support Consortium (INTASC), operating under the aegis of the Council of Chief State School Officers (CCSSO). This consortium of states has taken a leading role in developing beginning teacher standards that define a common knowledge base for teaching, based on research on development, learning, curriculum, and teaching. As I describe in Chapter 2, preparing teachers in light of these standards can help to enhance teacher quality.

Teaching quality, as distinct from teacher quality, refers to strong instruction that enables a wide range of students to learn. Such instruction meets the demands of the discipline, the goals of instruction, and the needs of students in a particular context. Teaching quality is in part a function of teacher quality—teachers' knowledge, skills, and dispositions—but it is also strongly influenced by the context of instruction, including factors aside from what the teacher knows and can do.

Key to considerations of context are the curriculum and assessment systems that support teachers' work, the "fit" between teachers' qualifications and what they are asked to teach, and teaching conditions. An excellent teacher may not be able to offer high-quality instruction in a context where he or she is asked to teach a flawed curriculum or lacks appropriate materials. Similarly, a well-prepared teacher may perform poorly when asked to teach outside the field of his or her preparation or under poor teaching conditions—for example, without adequate teaching materials, in substandard space, with too little time, or with classes that are far too large. Conversely, a less skilled teacher may be buoyed up by excellent materials, strong peer support for lesson planning, and additional specialists who work with students who may, for example, need extra help to learn to read.

The extent to which teachers experience dissimilar teaching conditions—and students have very different learning conditions—has been made clear in the school finance lawsuits brought forth in many states, which describe in vivid terms the differences between rich schools and poor schools. In the *Williams v. California* lawsuit, for example, teachers, parents, and students from low-income communities described overcrowded schools that had to run multiple shifts each day and multiple shifts during the school year, alternating on-and-off months for different cohorts of students cycling in and out of the building; classrooms with more than 40 students and not enough desks, chairs, and textbooks for each student to have one; lack of curriculum materials, science equipment, computers, and libraries; and crumbling facilities featuring leaky ceilings and falling ceiling tiles, sometimes overrun with rodents, and lacking heat and air conditioning. Not surprisingly, these under-resourced schools also had high levels of teacher turnover, making it difficult to create a coherent curriculum or develop common practices to support student learning.[13]

These kinds of conditions can undermine the effectiveness of any teacher. As one California teacher noted about a high-turnover school:

> "Hawthorne" was a difficult place to work. It was a very big school. The multi-track year-round schedule [requiring teachers to pack up their classrooms every few months and leave them and their students to return a month or so later] was very hard on teachers. The poor condition of the facilities made it an uncomfortable place to teach. Teachers who had to rove [from classroom to classroom]... found that so detrimental to the teaching process and the learning process and the professional growth process that they did not want to continue to have to work in that environment.[14]

Even where teachers have equivalent skills, there is little doubt that the quality of instruction experienced by students is greater in a school with high-quality and plentiful books, materials, and computers; a coherent, well-designed curriculum that teachers have built together; well-lit, properly heated, and generously outfitted classrooms; small class sizes; and instructional specialists than it is when students must learn in overcrowded, unsafe

> **Poor conditions can undermine the effectiveness of any teacher.**

> **If teaching is to be effective, policies that construct the learning environment and the teaching context must be addressed along with the qualities of individual teachers.**

conditions with insufficient materials, poorly chosen curriculum, large classes, and no instructional supports.[15]

Strong teacher quality may heighten the probability of effective teaching, but does not guarantee it. Initiatives to develop teaching quality and effectiveness must consider not only how to identify, reward, and use teachers' skills and abilities, but also how to develop teaching contexts that enable good practice. If teaching is to be effective, the policies that construct the learning environment and the teaching context must be addressed along with the qualities of individual teachers.

A SYSTEMIC APPROACH TO EVALUATING AND SUPPORTING TEACHING

It is clear that we need a more systemic approach to building and sustaining teacher effectiveness. Despite the apparent single-minded emphasis on teacher evaluation from some policy quarters, the importance of a more comprehensive approach is gaining currency. For example, in *Gearing Up: Creating a Systemic Approach to Teacher Effectiveness,* a recent task force of the National Association of State Boards of Education emphasized the importance of creating a more aligned system, beginning with recruitment and preparation and continuing through evaluation and career development.[16]

A high-quality teacher evaluation *system* should create a coherent, well-grounded approach to developing teaching, created collectively by state and district leaders with teachers and their representatives. In addition to clear standards for student learning, accompanied by high-quality curriculum materials and assessments, this system should include five key elements:

1. **Common statewide standards** for teaching that are related to meaningful student learning and are shared across the profession;

2. **Performance-based assessments, based on these standards,** guiding state functions, such as teacher preparation, licensure, and advanced certification;
3. **Local evaluation systems aligned to the same standards,** for evaluating on-the-job teaching based on multiple measures of teaching practice and student learning;
4. **Support structures** to ensure properly trained evaluators, mentoring for teachers who need additional assistance, and fair decisions about personnel actions; and
5. **Aligned professional learning opportunities** that support the improvement of teachers and teaching quality.

Based on research and evidence of best practices, the following chapters examine how each of these five elements should operate within a system that supports effective teaching and learning.

2 Start with Standards

To me, evaluations before [this] system were absolutely meaningless. . . . There was no standard to base it on. There was no sense of growth. . . . I think using the CSTPs (California Standards for the Teaching Profession) has been great. Because if you look at those standards . . . I mean, if I could do all of those things I'd be great! It's daunting. But it's given people a better sense of what teaching is in a broader sense.

—*Greg Jouriles, Teacher and Association Leader, San Mateo, California*

"If you don't know where you are going, any road will take you there," observed the Cheshire Cat in *Alice in Wonderland.* So it is in education. Without a clear understanding of what students should learn and how teaching can support them, it is easy to wander aimlessly. Developing a shared vision of educational goals and supportive instruction is the foundation for a system that can support effective teaching.

In this chapter, I take up the initial stepping stones for a comprehensive system: First is the importance of starting with standards for student learning that represent meaningful goals for what students should learn and be able to do. And second is the importance of aligning these to standards for teaching that can guide assessments of teaching in a continuous way throughout the entire career: from preservice through initial licensure, induction, professional licensure, and recognition of accomplished practice.

STANDARDS FOR STUDENT LEARNING

Most nations (or states within large nations) have adopted common frameworks for curriculum that articulate the topics and skills students should learn. These are used to guide instructional planning and teacher development, as well as assessments of students. Learning standards and curriculum frameworks were also developed by most U.S. states during the 1990s, often guided by the work of associations like the National Councils of Teachers of English and Mathematics, among others in the content areas. These were useful in helping to organize educational efforts; however, the standards documents in many states became diffuse and often overstuffed, leaving many with a curriculum characterized as a mile wide and an inch deep.

The Common Core State Standards (CCSS), which more than 45 states have recently adopted, are a new effort to achieve a more common vision of educational purpose. The CCSS seek to provide "fewer, clearer, and higher" expectations for learning across the grade levels in English language arts and mathematics. These standards are intended to provide guidance for understanding how students learn in a progressive fashion along skill strands, as well as what should be taught to enable them to be both college- and career-ready by the end of high school. The standards aim to ensure that students have developed the capacity to read and listen critically for understanding; to write and speak clearly and persuasively, with reference to evidence; and to calculate and communicate mathematically, reason quantitatively, and design solutions to complex problems.

The Common Core Standards will also require a more integrated approach to delivering content instruction across all subject areas. The English language arts standards are written to include the development of critical reading, writing, speaking, and listening skills in history, science, mathematics, and the arts as well as in English class. The mathematics standards are written to include the use of mathematical skills and concepts in fields such as science, technology, and engineering. These standards emphasize the ways in which students should use literacy and numeracy skills across the curriculum and in life.

The CCSS are not perfect: In their first iteration, they did not always achieve the goal of parsimony they set out to attain; they have posited learning progressions in how knowledge and skills are acquired across the grades that may turn out to need considerable refinement; and they have been critiqued regarding their developmental appropriateness, especially for the very early grades, as well as their responsiveness to what is known about language acquisition for new English learners and other students.

However, they offer a productive vision for what students should know and be able to do to be college- and career-ready when they finish high school, and a useful starting point from which educators can refine curriculum plans over time. Nations that have developed national curricula—like Finland, Japan, Singapore, and South Korea—along with states or provinces in larger countries that have articulated a curriculum design for their jurisdictions—like Victoria, Australia; Ontario, Canada; and Shanghai, China—see these statements as living documents that are continually revised to address needs and meet new challenges.

States that have not adopted the Common Core Standards are seeking to accomplish similar goals in state-developed standards. As states seek to implement these standards, they must also rethink their curriculum frameworks, materials, and assessments, so that they support these skills and enable them to be well taught. This will require more emphasis on higher-order thinking skills and abilities; more extensive inquiry, complex problem solving, writing, discussion, research and presentation of data, and other forms of communication in classrooms; and more open-ended assessments calling for applications of these skills.

> **The Common Core Standards will require more higher-order thinking; inquiry, complex problem solving, writing, discussion, research and presentation of data, and other forms of communication in classrooms; and more open-ended assessments.**

Changes in assessment will be a major aspect of implementing new "college- and career-ready" standards. Current state tests overwhelmingly test lower-level skills in multiple-choice formats. According to a recent RAND Corporation study that analyzed test items across states,[1] only 2% of math items and 21% of English language arts items on current state tests measure deeper learning objectives. These objectives include such higher-level skills as the abilities to apply concepts, analyze, synthesize, critique, prove, and design.[2]

By contrast, the Content Specifications for the new assessments being developed by two recently established multistate assessment consortia (the Smarter Balanced Assessment Consortium [SBAC] and the Partnership for Assessment and Research of the Common Core [PARCC]) plan to assess all students on these deeper learning skills,[3] more than doubling the emphasis on higher-order skills in English language arts tasks and increasing the number of items assessing such skills by more than ten-fold in mathematics. Assessments will include more open-ended items and expect students to apply their skills to real-world problems and explain what they have learned. In performance tasks for SBAC states, for example, students will be expected to research a topic on the Internet, such as the pros and cons of building a nuclear power plant, collect and evaluate evidence about it, and write a well-grounded essay explaining complex information or arguing for a particular course of action. They will also analyze and use quantitative data to inform a decision they must make or a design they must accomplish, such as planning a field trip based on costs, distance, and student preferences, or designing a planter for the school atrium.

Clearly there will be substantial learning needs for teachers and administrators as they develop and implement these new curricula and assessments, and as they seek to transform teaching and the organization of schools.

Nations or states that have articulated such core curriculum expectations have typically produced sets of standards, curriculum supports, and associated assessments that provide an essential context for teacher development and evaluation. A major part of teachers' ongoing professional learning takes place as they develop, in collaboration with their colleagues, the specific lessons and assessment tools they will use in the classroom. These collaborative learning opportunities can become very analytic and intensive through the use of strategies such as Lesson Study in Japan, action research about practice in Finland, and Learning Circles in Singapore (see box: Japanese Lesson Study). These collaborations enlighten the efforts of all of the participating teachers while at the same time setting expectations about how core curriculum topics can be well taught and well learned.

JAPANESE LESSON STUDY

In Japan, *kenkyuu jugyou* (research lessons) help develop well-grounded approaches to teaching the national curriculum and are a key part of the learning culture for teachers. Every teacher periodically prepares a best possible lesson that demonstrates strategies to achieve a specific goal (e.g., students becoming active problem-solvers or students learning more from each other) in collaboration with other colleagues. A group of teachers observes while the lesson is taught and usually records the lesson in a number of ways, including videotapes, audiotapes, and narrative and/or checklist observations that focus on areas of interest to the instructing teacher (e.g., how many students volunteered their own ideas). Afterward, the group of teachers, and sometimes outside educators, will discuss the lesson's strengths and weakness, ask questions, and make suggestions for how to improve the lesson. In some cases the revised lesson is given by another teacher only a few days later and observed and discussed again.

Teachers themselves decide the theme and frequency of research lessons. Large study groups often break up into subgroups of four to six teachers. The subgroups plan their own lessons but work toward the same goal, and teachers from all subgroups share and comment on lessons and try to attend the lessons and follow-up discussions. For a typical lesson study, the 10 to 15 hours of group meetings are spread over 3 to 4 weeks. Although the school day ends for students between 2:40 and 3:45 p.m., teachers' work days don't end until 5:00 p.m., which provides additional time for collegial work and planning. Most lesson study meetings occur during the hours after school lets out.

The research lessons allow teachers to refine individual lessons, consult with other teachers, and receive feedback based on colleagues' observations of their classroom practice, reflect on their own practice, learn new content and approaches, and build a culture that emphasizes continuous improvement and collaboration. Some teachers also provide public research lessons, a practice that expedites the spread of best practices across schools; allows principals, district personnel, and policymakers to see how teachers are grappling with new subject matter and goals; and gives the field greater access to the work of excellent teachers.[4]

STANDARDS FOR TEACHING

While standards for student learning help focus attention on what is to be taught, standards for teaching help focus our attention on how instructional efforts can be effective. The National Board for

Professional Teaching Standards (NBPTS), created in 1987 and comprised of highly respected classroom teachers, along with other educators and members of the public, was the first professional body to create benchmarks for how accomplished veteran teachers can enact the kind of learning envisioned by student learning standards.

Much like board certification in medicine, the NBPTS mission is to "establish high and rigorous standards for what accomplished teachers should know and be able to do, to develop and operate a voluntary national system to assess and certify teachers who meet those standards, and to advance related education reforms—all with the purpose of improving student learning."[5]

The standards developed by the National Board are subject specific and keyed to the developmental level of students, from early childhood to early adulthood. Standards in more than 30 areas incorporate knowledge about teaching and learning that supports a view of teaching as complex, contingent on students' needs and instructional goals, and reciprocal—that is, continually shaped and reshaped by students' responses to learning events.

Since the early 1990s, more than 100,000 teachers have achieved National Board Certification, representing about 3% of the nation's teaching force. In many locations, these teachers have become master or mentor teachers, teacher educators, or leaders at the classroom or school level. But the influence of the National Board has been even greater.

These standards have been critically important to the development of more accurate and useful teacher evaluation because they instantiate the findings of decades of research in descriptions of practice—illustrating what effective teachers *know and do* to promote learning.

The NBPTS standards have informed standards for beginning teacher preparation and licensing and, in a few places, standards for inservice evaluation as well. They stimulated the creation of the beginning-teacher licensing standards developed by the Interstate New Teacher Assessment and Support Consortium (INTASC, 1992), adopted by more than 40 states as the basis for licensing teachers and approving programs.

Both NBPTS and INTASC standards are responsive to a multicultural and multilingual student body that includes diverse approaches to learning. By reflecting subject-matter standards for students, the demands of learner diversity, and the expectation that teachers must collaborate with colleagues and parents in order to succeed, the standards define teaching as a collegial, professional activity based on considerations of subjects and students. By examining teaching in the light of learning, they put considerations of effectiveness at the center of practice.

The National Board standards have also been important because they redefined teacher assessment. Rather than having teachers take a paper-and-pencil test or having observers use a checklist to tally a set of behaviors, the assessments closely examine the practice of teaching in relation to learning. To achieve National Board Certification, candidates must complete a portfolio that incorporates student work samples, videotapes of classroom practice, and extensive written analyses and reflections based upon these artifacts. The portfolio is meant to allow teachers to present a picture of their practice as it is shaped by the particular needs of the students with whom the teachers work and the particular context of each teacher's school.

The portfolio evidence is scored by trained raters who are expert in the same teaching field, using rubrics that define critical dimensions of teaching, such as planning based on knowledge of students' learning, instruction that uses effective strategies responsive to students' needs, and assessment and feedback that allow students to improve their work.

> **National Board standards have redefined teacher assessment by closely examining the practice of teaching in relation to learning.**

This process of studying the standards and seeking to meet them has inspired many teachers to improve their practice in ways that they feel are long lasting. As a Board Certified English teacher noted:

> The National Board standards articulate a vision for accomplished teaching that I had suspected existed but had never before seen in one place. The National Board standards and process honor the teaching profession by presenting a provocative expectation for what it means to be excellent. The certification process requires teachers to dig in so deeply to their rationale for instruction and assessment that one can't help but get better. It taught me what it means to be a truly reflective teacher.[6]

A survey of more than 5,600 National Board candidates found that 92% believe the National Board Certification process made them a better teacher, reporting that it helped them create stronger curricula, improved their abilities to evaluate student learning, and enhanced their interaction with students, parents, and other teachers.[7] National Board participants often say that they have learned more about teaching from their participation in the assessments than they have learned from any other previous professional development experience. Teacher David Haynes's statement is typical of many:

> Completing the portfolio for the Early Adolescence/Generalist Certification was, quite simply, the single most powerful professional development experience of my career. Never before have I thought so deeply about what I do with children, and why I do it. I looked critically at my practice, judging it against a set of high and rigorous standards. Often in daily work, I found myself rethinking my goals, correcting my course, moving in new directions. I am not the same teacher as I was before the assessment, and my experience seems to be typical.[8]

Not only do teachers appear to learn as they go through the certification process, those who are involved in scoring the assessments using rubrics that incorporate the standards also feel they learn about good teaching. Similar assessments recently developed for beginning teachers, based on the INTASC standards, have also proved useful for both evaluating effectiveness and improving practice.

One reason these standards seem to promote productive learning through the evaluation process is that they are expressed in performance terms—that is, they describe what teachers should know, be like, and be able to do rather than listing courses that teachers should take in order to be awarded a license or certificate. This shift toward performance-based standard-setting is in line with the approach to licensing and certification taken in other professions and with the changes already occurring in a number of states. This approach aims to clarify what the criteria are for determining competence.

> The shift toward performance-based standard-setting is in line with the approach to licensing and certification taken in other professions.

A second reason these standards appear to be educative is that they are evaluated authentically, through evidence of actual performance, rather than through proxies that are further removed from what people really *do* with the knowledge and skills they acquire.

Despite these advances, there has been remarkably little effort to connect these standards to districts' on-the-job evaluations of teachers. Local teacher evaluations vary widely across districts, and are often based on checklists of teacher behaviors that are not associated with effectiveness. As noted teaching researcher Mary Kennedy remarked:

> The evaluations themselves are typically of little value—a single, fleeting classroom visit by a principal or other building administrator untrained in evaluation, wielding a checklist of classroom conditions and teacher behaviors that often don't even focus directly on the quality of teacher instruction. It's typically a couple of dozen items on a list: "Is presentably dressed," "Starts on time," "Room is safe," "The lesson occupies students". . . . But, in most instances, it's nothing more than marking "satisfactory" or "unsatisfactory."[9]

Even as professional standards have been evolving at the state and national level, they have been ignored by many local districts. Thus, teachers encounter a wide variety of disjointed signals over the course of a career, and opportunities to develop high-quality practice are missed at every turn. A comprehensive approach to teacher evaluation would create more useful standards-based assessments for state licensure and advanced certification, and would then use these same standards as a framework for more meaningful local evaluations that occur on the job.

> **Teachers encounter a wide variety of disjointed signals over the course of a career.**

In the next chapter (Chapter 3), I describe what states could do to create a standards-based framework for evaluating teaching along the continuum from preparation and licensing through induction, professional learning, and advanced certification. In Chapter 4, I describe how local districts could create complementary systems of local evaluation that support assessment and development on an ongoing basis, enabling growth over the course of the teaching career.

3 Create a Continuum of Performance Assessments

Many times since [becoming National Board Certified], I have thought about these two polar experiences [the National Board assessment and my local district evaluation process]. I feel they shine a light on key inadequacies of the current [local district] evaluation process that might be thoughtfully improved. In order to be effectively implemented, the [local district] process needs to reflect meaningfully the performance of teachers at every level—from the weakest, who must be identified for assistance or dismissal—to the superior, who deserve recognition for their exemplary roles in our schools. The media frequently clamor about getting rid of "bad teachers," which taints us all. Meanwhile, many of our most outstanding teachers work tirelessly year in and year out with little official recognition or reward for their efforts.

— Jane Fung, National Board Certified Teacher, Los Angeles, California

In her reflection above, master teacher Jane Fung notes that the benefit of the National Board portfolio assessment is that, unlike her local district evaluation process, it actually measures teaching performance. She also notes that the critical issue for improving evaluation in general is developing systems that can meaningfully assess the performance of teachers at every level—from novice to expert, and from struggling teachers to those who are highly accomplished. To do this, we will need to ensure that assessments of performance can operate along a continuum that reflects practice from entry-level through mastery.

FEATURES OF PERFORMANCE ASSESSMENTS

What does it take to measure performance well? And what would it take to establish a performance-based system applicable throughout the teaching career?

Standards are nothing but words on a piece of paper until they are translated into expectations and actions guiding what students and teachers actually *do* on behalf of learning. Researchers have found that well-designed performance-based assessments:

1. **Capture teaching in action**, by looking at classroom practice in terms of what both teachers and students are doing to achieve particular learning goals;
2. **Observe and assess aspects of teaching related to teachers' effectiveness**, such as activating and building on students' prior knowledge, creating appropriate scaffolds to support the steps of the learning process, and creating opportunities for students to apply their knowledge, receive feedback, and revise their work;
3. **Examine teachers' intentions and strategies** for meeting the needs of particular students and the demands of the subject matter being taught;
4. **Look at teaching in relation to student learning** by evaluating student work that results from teaching, plus teachers' feedback and support that further improves student work; and
5. **Use rubrics that vividly describe performance standards** at different levels of expertise to evaluate teachers' practices, strategies, and outcomes.[1]

Performance assessments with these features include those used for National Board Certification and for beginning teacher licensure in states such as Connecticut, California, and others now piloting a national version of such a portfolio (discussed later in this chapter). They also include the standards-based teacher evaluation systems used in some local districts (discussed further in Chapter 4).

> **On-the-job evaluations have often used checklists that do not examine teaching and learning in meaningful ways.**

It is high time for this change. For many decades, teachers have been licensed based on scores on traditional paper-and-pencil tests of basic skills and subject matter, which, although perhaps useful for establishing academic standards, have not been significantly related to effectiveness in the classroom.[2] And on-the-job evaluations have often used checklists that do not examine teaching and learning in meaningful ways. However, in a significant breakthrough, recent well-designed performance-based assessments have been found to measure aspects of teaching related to teachers' effectiveness, as measured by their students' progress.

For example, a number of studies have found that the National Board Certification assessment process distinguishes teachers who are more effective in improving student achievement from others who do not achieve certification.[3] Similarly, beginning teachers' ratings on the Connecticut BEST assessments were found to predict their students' achievement gains on state tests, whereas other measures—such as undergraduate college, grade point average, and traditional tests of subject-matter knowledge or basic skills—did not.[4] The scores of entering teachers on the Performance Assessment for California Teachers (PACT) have also been found to predict their students' gains on state tests.[5]

All of these performance assessments are portfolios that collect evidence of teachers' actual instruction, through videotapes, curriculum plans, and samples of student work and learning, along with teacher commentaries explaining the basis for teachers' decisions about what and how they taught, in light of their curriculum goals and student needs, and how they assessed learning and gave feedback to individual students.

When these kinds of assessments are used to guide teaching and provide teachers with feedback, researchers have found that teachers are able to improve their skills. And participation in these assessments supports learning both for teachers who are being evaluated and for educators who are trained to serve as evaluators. Thus, the assessments both *document* and help teachers *develop* greater effectiveness. In addition, they create a common language and set of understandings about good teaching for the field as a whole.

CREATING A STATE SYSTEM

Ideally, to create a coherent system, states would develop a tiered licensure system that licenses new teachers and recognizes accomplished teachers based on their demonstrated performance. The system would frame a career continuum for professional learning and advancement to which local evaluations are aligned. For teacher evaluation to make sense across the continuum of the career, it should:

- Begin with common standards, like those of INTASC, and performance assessments for *initial licensing* (often called the preliminary or tier 1 license) that reflect the knowledge and skills needed to teach effectively;
- Use these same standards to guide *induction* for beginning teachers and to shape the assessments of performance that determine the receipt of a *professional license* (often called a tier 2 license);
- Determine *tenure* at the district level based on these standards, with tenure understood, as it generally is in state laws, as the granting of due process rights to teachers—ensuring that a teacher cannot be dismissed without cause—rather than as a lifetime guarantee to a job;
- Build local evaluation systems and professional learning opportunities for *ongoing assessment and development* around the same standards, so that teacher development is coherent and consistent across the career; and
- Create opportunities for *recognition and advancement*— including new roles that allow teachers to spread their expertise to others—using complementary standards and assessments of accomplished practice, like those of the National Board. In some states this is considered a third tier of the licensure system, as shown in Figure 3.1.

Figure 3.1: A Continuum of Teacher Performance Assessment

TIER 3
Assessment for Advanced Certification

- After tenure of professional license
- Assessment of accomplishment as an experienced teacher
- National Board Certifications or state/local alternative
- Evidence used for differentiated compensation and leadership roles

TIER 2
Assessment for Professional Licensing

- Following induction, prior to tenure
- Systematic collection of evidence about teacher practice and student learning
- Evidence also used to inform mentoring and professional development

TIER 1
Assessment for Initial Licensing

- At entry to profession
- A common high standard of practice for all pathways (preservice, internships, and alternate routes)
- Coupled with assessment of content knowledge
- Evidence used for program approval and accreditation

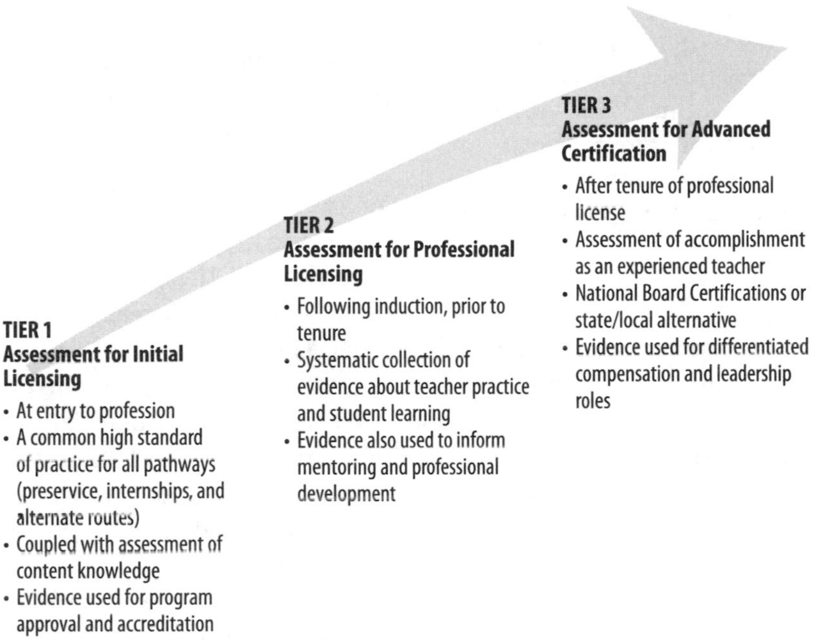

Building a Strong Foundation for Entry

Tier 1: The Initial License. To leverage stronger preparation and teacher quality, states should make initial licensing decisions based on performance-based evidence of teacher competence. Since the 1980s, the desire for greater confidence in licensing decisions has led to the introduction of teacher licensing tests in nearly all states. However, these tests—generally multiple-choice tests of basic skills and subject matter—do not predict teachers' abilities to effectively teach children. They may be appropriate as a screening test for domain knowledge, but not to determine who is fully able to teach. Furthermore, in many cases, these tests evaluate teachers' knowledge *before* they enter or complete teacher education, and hence are an inadequate tool for teacher education accountability.

By contrast, in states that have already used them, performance assessments of beginning teachers have been found not only to

> **Performance assessments not only measure features of teaching associated with effectiveness, but actually help develop effectiveness at the same time—both for the participants and for the programs that prepare them.**

measure features of teaching associated with effectiveness, but actually to help develop effectiveness at the same time—both for the participants and for the programs that prepare them.

Established professions such as medicine, nursing, and law have long had state tests for licensure that are designed by members of the profession through their state professional standards boards. The bar exam in law, which requires lawyers to demonstrate that they can analyze cases, cite precedent, and write legal memoranda or briefs, is a familiar example. In the medical licensing examination, prospective doctors must be able to accurately diagnose patients and prescribe medical interventions in simulations that can evaluate the likely outcomes for patients. Candidates for the Architectural Registration exam submit a portfolio of their work that includes certain specified elements, not unlike the portfolio required by the National Board for Professional Teaching Standards and more recent assessments for beginning teachers.

The examinations in other professions differ from most traditional teacher licensing tests in two ways: First, although they are administered by testing companies, they are designed and developed by members of the profession. Second, they assess readiness to practice at least in part through tasks that are authentic representations of what professionals do. These professional examinations are, in these respects, similar to the recently developed performance assessments of beginning teachers used in states such as California and Connecticut. These teacher performance assessments have been developed by members of the profession to include authentic elements of teaching-in-action. As noted earlier, they have been found to both measure features of teaching associated with effectiveness and help develop participant and program effectiveness at the same time.

Teachers who have experienced the power of performance assessments have consistently confirmed that this approach to

> **Teachers who have experienced the power of performance assessments have consistently confirmed that this approach to evaluation is highly useful to them.**

evaluation is highly useful to them. So it has been with California's PACT, which was built by teacher educators and teachers from across the state and is used by more than 30 traditional and alternative programs for initial teacher licensing. As a teacher educator at one of those universities (Stanford University), I have personally seen how the PACT has helped to strengthen preparation, providing us with a strong focus for helping our candidates synthesize their learning and useful information for reflecting on our program and continually strengthening its curriculum and clinical experiences. The involvement of instructors, supervisors, and cooperating teachers in supporting the PACT has also created a more common vision of teaching across the program.

Like our peers, we have seen that candidates report that they have learned more about teaching from completing the assessment. As one noted:

> For me, the most valuable thing was the sequencing of the lessons: teaching the lesson, and evaluating what the kids were getting, what they weren't getting, and having that be reflected in my next lesson . . . the "teach-assess-teach-assess-teach-assess" process. You're constantly changing: You may have a plan or a framework, but you know that has to be flexible, based on what the children learn that day.
>
> —A teaching candidate

University and school faculty score these portfolios using standardized rubrics; training and moderation processes, along with an audit procedure, help to calibrate standards and ensure reliability. Faculties then use the PACT results to revise their curricula. The scoring participants describe how this process creates a shared understanding of good teaching, focuses them on how to improve preparation, and creates a foundation for planning teacher induction and professional development.

This [scoring] experience . . . has forced me to revisit the question of what really matters in the assessment of teachers, which—in turn—means revisiting the question of what really matters in the preparation of teachers.

—A teacher education faculty member

[The scoring process] forces you to be clear about "good teaching"—what it looks like, sounds like. It enables you to look at your own practice critically, with new eyes.

—A cooperating teacher

As an induction program coordinator, I have a much clearer picture of what credential holders will bring to us and of what they'll be required to do. We can build on this.

—An induction program coordinator

The process not only helps teachers and evaluators to grow, it reaps additional benefits as data are fed back to teacher preparation programs. PACT programs receive detailed, aggregated data on all of their candidates by program area and dimensions of teaching—such as planning, instruction, assessment, reflection, and the development of academic language—and use the data to improve their curriculum, instruction, and program designs. Using these aggregated data for accreditation can ultimately provide a solid basis for reviewing programs with an eye toward their outcomes in preparing candidates to demonstrate they can actually teach. With the addition of incentives for National Board Certification later in the career, these assessments would provide a continuum of measures that both identify and help stimulate increasing effectiveness across the worklife of a teacher.

This approach to assessment has been at the heart of recent recommendations from both national teacher associations. In its report *Transforming Teaching*, the National Education Association called for a career continuum based on nationally established professional teaching standards that guide preparation and teacher performance assessments completed before licensure.[6] In *Raising the Bar*, the American Federation of Teachers called for a "bar exam" for teaching that offers a nationally available performance assessment for licensure, along with evidence of competence in the subject area and strong clinical training.[7]

Currently, building on the experience of the PACT, more than 25 states and nearly 200 preparation programs have joined together in a Teacher Performance Assessment Consortium (TPAC)[8] to create a common version of an initial licensing assessment, the edTPA, which can be used nationwide to make preparation and licensing performance-based and grounded in teachers' abilities to support student learning. This new teacher performance assessment, recently piloted with 7,000 candidates in more than 160 programs across 22 states, is based on teaching standards that are linked to the Common Core State Standards, which will ultimately be embedded in states' curriculum frameworks. The assessment ensures that teachers-in-training can plan, teach, and evaluate student learning effectively (see Table 3.1).

Amee Adkins, teacher educator and associate dean at Illinois State University, notes: "If there's one positive outcome from the current aggressive rhetoric aimed at teachers and teacher preparation, it is the [edTPA]. It offers an opportunity to shift the paradigm from a license as an entitlement for completing a curriculum to an obligation to demonstrate the proficiency the curriculum intends."[9]

> **Universities are finding that the assessment helps candidates as well as teacher educators improve their practice.**

Universities are finding that the assessment helps candidates as well as teacher educators improve their practice. In Ohio, 32 institutions piloted all or part of the TPAC assessment in 2010–2011 and studied the outcomes. When teaching candidates who took the assessment were surveyed, 96% had positive comments about the experience, pointing to the fact that the assessment helped them acquire new learning and become more self-aware, and that it focused their attention on student learning.[10]

Candidates observed of the assessment:

> It really made me analyze what I did or why I thought the way I did. I know that as a teacher there are always ways I can improve, but when I am forced to put everything down on paper and to support why I chose to do what I did, I see where my strengths and weaknesses are.

Table 3.1: Teacher Performance Assessment, Elementary Literacy Portfolio

Assessment Components	Evidence Submitted
Task 1: Planning Instruction and Assessment	

• Provide relevant information about your instructional context.
• Select a learning segment of 3–5 sequential lessons that teach literacy skills and strategies and support students to comprehend and/or compose text.
• Create an instruction and assessment plan for the learning segment that focuses on a key literacy concept and considers your students' strengths and needs.
• Explain what you know about your students and the thinking behind your plans.
• Make daily notes about the effectiveness of your teaching for your students' learning.
	☐ Information About the Learning Context
	☐ Lesson Plans for Learning Segment
	  • Lesson Plans
	  • Instructional Materials
	  • Assessment Tools/ Procedures and Criteria
	☐ Planning Commentary

Task 2: Instructing and Engaging Students in Learning	
• Submit video clips from lessons where you engage your students to develop literacy strategies to comprehend and/or compose text. • Analyze your teaching and your students' learning in the video clips.	☐ Video Clip(s) ☐ Instruction Commentary
Task 3: Assessing Student Learning	
• Analyze class performance from one assessment completed during the learning segment. Identify three student work samples that illustrate trends in student understanding within the class.	☐ Student Work Samples ☐ Evidence of Feedback ☐ Assessment Commentary

Assessment Components	Evidence Submitted
• Select and analyze the learning of two focus students in more depth, and document your feedback on their work. • Provide the assessment task and evaluation criteria.	
Task 4: Analyzing Teaching	
• Using notes you have recorded throughout the learning segment, respond to commentary prompts to explain what you have learned about your teaching practice and two or three things you would do differently if you could teach the learning segment over. Explain why the changes would improve your students' learning.	☐ Analyzing Teaching Commentary
Task 5: Academic Language in Literacy (evidence is gathered across tasks as noted)	
• Select one key language demand related to the literacy central focus. Explain how you will support students with varied language needs. • Cite evidence of opportunities for students to understand and use the targeted academic language in: (1) the video clips from the Instruction task, OR (2) the student work samples from the Assessment task. • Analyze the effectiveness of your language supports.	☐ Planning Commentary ☐ Instruction Commentary ☐ Assessment Commentary

> [It helped me] because I was analyzing student learning and developing lessons that met the needs of each individual student. It helped me develop lessons that were within the students' ability level, but pushed them to think more in depth.

> The process was very educational. My cooperating teacher read over my task and commented that it was great to have student teachers do this assessment. I learned a lot about myself and my planning and how I can reflect on it and continue to grow.

Teacher educators also felt the process was educative both for their students and for themselves:

> It forced the teacher candidates to examine what they were doing as beginning teachers. It also forced me to look at the materials that I was including in my seminar and the relevance of these materials to my students.

Marcy Singer Gabella, a teacher educator at Vanderbilt University, notes that faculty at the eight Tennessee universities piloting the assessment say that working with the edTPA has led to more productive conversations about how to develop strong teaching practices. She adds that edTPA-related changes are resulting in noticeable differences in its graduates' readiness for the field. For example, early work with the assessment revealed that candidates were having difficulty analyzing student work and giving students usable feedback. In response, Vanderbilt teacher education faculty revised coursework and field assignments to provide more opportunities for practice in these areas.[11]

Vanderbilt student teacher Nicole Renner remarked that the edTPA really changed her capacity to teach by refocusing her from herself—where most beginners start—to the students. Nicole noted that:

> Even though the TPA is used for summative assessment, it is also formative, and the main lesson of the TPA is exactly what new and pre-service teachers need to learn: it's about the students, dummy. . . . (T)he TPA process shape(s) the candidate's field experience in meaningful ways that specifically address changing the candidate's focus to be entirely on

students. Yes, we videotape lessons, and we refer to that as "videotaping *ourselves*," but what we are really trying to capture on that tape is our ability to foster a student-centered learning experience.[12]

Nicole's graphic summary of how the edTPA changes the typical student-teaching experience is shown in Table 3.2. It illustrates vividly how a well-constructed performance assessment can be a critical gift in helping novices become professional teachers.

By 2013, the edTPA will be nationally available for use in initial licensing or for programs that want to develop useful outcome data for accreditation.

Table 3.2: How a Teacher Performance Assessment Can Change Student Teaching

"Typical" Student Teaching	edTPA Experience
Day-to-day focus, sometimes with no accountability for extended planning, especially if the cooperating teacher is the type to "fly by the seat of her pants"	Emphasis on long-term planning WITH mid-course corrections and daily adjustments
Observation of isolated lessons	Records an arc of instruction
About teacher behaviors	About student work
Evaluation of teaching led by outside observers (cooperating teacher, university supervisor, etc.)	Self-led evaluation of teaching (with appropriate guidance and feedback)
Difficult to focus on individual students • Don't know students well • Cooperating teachers may not do it	Requires focus on individual students at different performance levels
More about rehearsal of teaching practices than assessment of teaching readiness	High stakes—just like solo teaching!
Multitude of inputs regarding "good" teaching practice from coursework and field interactions	Unified vision of core competencies for effective teaching, encountered during actual teaching practice

Source: Nicole Renner (2012).

Tier II: The Professional License. A more advanced version of the assessment, similar to one originally built in Connecticut and another currently under development in Ohio, could also be used at the point of the professional license (at the end of the probationary period, usually after 3 years), and to guide the mentoring process during the induction period.

As noted earlier, the BEST portfolio in Connecticut, used with 2nd-year teachers, was found in a study to be the only one of several teacher qualifications (including traditional licensing tests and academic preparation indicators) to predict teachers' effectiveness with students. As with the preservice performance assessments discussed earlier, it helped novices improve their practice. A beginning teacher in Connecticut who participated in the BEST assessment described the power of the process, which required him to plan and teach a unit and to reflect daily on the day's lesson, considering how the lesson met the needs of each student and what should be changed in the next day's plans. He noted:

> The BEST portfolio in Connecticut, used with 2nd-year teachers, was found in a study to be the only one of several teacher qualifications to predict teachers' effectiveness.

> Although I was the reflective type anyway, it made me go a step further. I would have to say, okay, this is how I'm going to do it differently. It made more of an impact on my teaching and was more beneficial to me than just one lesson in which you state what you're going to do. . . . The process makes you think about your teaching and reflect on your teaching. And I think that's necessary to become an effective teacher.[13]

More than 40 states currently require some form of induction for beginning teachers, but these programs are rarely guided by a clear vision of what teachers should be able to do by the end of that period. Because the professional license is generally granted just before tenure decisions are made by local districts, this assessment could inform those decisions as well.

> States and districts that have adopted performance assessments to guide induction have supported much more purposeful and focused mentoring.

States and districts that have adopted performance assessments to guide induction and decisions about licensing and tenure have supported much more purposeful and focused mentoring, with greater attention to a shared vision of good practice.

Developing Accomplished Practice

Tier III: Advanced Recognition. As described in the previous chapter, National Board Certification has been used by a number of states to trigger salary increases and other forms of teacher recognition, such as selection as a mentor or lead teacher. In addition to the fact that National Board Certification is associated with teacher effectiveness, it also helps already-competent teachers to continue to improve. This is a critical new expectation for assessments. To support a stronger profession, we should insist that evaluation processes both measure effectiveness well and help develop stronger practice.

Many studies have found that teachers' participation in the National Board process supports their professional learning and stimulates changes in their practice. Teachers note that the process of analyzing their own and their students' work in light of standards enables them to better assess student learning. It also helps them to evaluate the effects of their own actions and change them when necessary. Finally, teachers often develop new practices that are called for in the standards and assessments, such as leading classroom discussions, organizing group work, conducting investigations in science, or engaging students in a writing process.[14] Teachers report significant improvements in their performance in each area assessed—planning, designing, and delivering instruction; managing the classroom; diagnosing and evaluating student learning; using subject-matter knowledge; and participating in a learning community—and studies have documented that these changes do indeed occur.[15]

> **Teachers' analysis of their own and their students' work in light of standards enables them to evaluate the effects of their actions and change them when necessary.**

Some schools have taken advantage of the learning stimulated by National Board Certification to create a whole-school improvement strategy by encouraging all of the teachers to engage in Board Certification at the same time. The introduction of this educative approach to assessment has proved successful in greatly improving teachers' practice and student achievement. (See Box: How National Board Assessment Can Turn a School Around.)

HOW NATIONAL BOARD ASSESSMENT CAN TURN A SCHOOL AROUND

School-wide participation in National Board Certification can help teachers build their collective, as well as individual, effectiveness. For example, the turnaround strategy at once-failing and now-much-improved Mitchell Elementary School in Phoenix, Arizona, was to increase teacher expertise using the National Board Certification process, supported by the Elementary and Secondary Education Act's Title II funding. In this low-income Latino community, where most students are English language learners, more than 60% of the teachers—most of whom are from the community and reflect their student population—are either National Board Certified or in the process of earning certification. Mitchell teachers claim the National Board process transformed the school, as they have worked collectively to better understand their teaching. Not only has the school's achievement dramatically improved, but teacher turnover is no longer a problem.[16] As the district's associate superintendent, Suzanne Zentner, noted, "We believe in the National Board Certification process as an approach to . . . closing the achievement gap."[17]

A similar strategy transformed Julius Corsini Elementary School in Palm Springs, California—a high-poverty school serving 90% Latino students, 85% of whom are English learners. When Keila Bonelli, a National Board Certified teacher, arrived as principal in 2006, the school had been in Program Improvement status for 4 years, and teacher turnover rates had reached 75% a year. At her urging, all 45 teachers at the school undertook the National Board Certification process, either by doing an initial portfolio entry, through the "Take One" option, or by beginning work on a full portfolio. The Take One cohort, along with the principal and assistant principal, all decided to do the entry for the English as a New Language certificate so they could jointly develop and reflect on these practices for teaching their English-learner students.

As the teachers examined their teaching in light of the standards, they also decided to work together on teaching writing more effectively and on using common teaching strategies, including Thinking Maps, to help students learn more efficiently. Many of the teachers successfully passed their entries and moved on to completing their portfolios. In the years that followed, the entire staff committed to becoming National Board Certified, a feat that would make them the first such staff in the state.

At the end of the 2006 school year, the school's Academic Performance Index (API) had improved by 55 points—a gain about 10 times greater than the state average. The school was one of five in the state to exit Program Improvement status that year. The following year, it again improved by nearly the same margin. Equally important, the school developed a strong professional culture, eliminated turnover, and became a magnet for other great teachers.

The standard teacher evaluation process also changed. With permission from the district and the union, the principal borrowed from the National Board process to pilot an alternative evaluation method that relies on writing records of teaching events and using them in conversation with teachers to identify strengths and needs. Teachers welcome this approach to evaluation and say that it is helping them continue to develop their practice in line with their National Board work.

Other schools across the country have experienced similar successes using this strategy in recent years. In a recent study of five such schools,[18] principals underscored the role of the National Board process in building a strong professional community in which teachers not only reflect on their own practice but also push one another to reflect more deeply. A principal noted that she now routinely sees teachers ask one another to justify reasons for their instructional choices. Another remarked on the significant change in the ways that teachers make sense of student performance data, underscoring that the school had always been "data driven," but now teachers are more likely to dig deeply and pose explanations for why they get the results they do. One district administrator said, "I have never heard teachers engage in this kind of deep reflection before."

A PERFORMANCE-BASED CONTINUUM IN ACTION:
THE CASE OF NEW MEXICO

A number of states have already begun to build a continuum of teacher performance assessments, as beginning teachers are evaluated using performance assessments for licensure and veteran teachers who are considered for lead teacher status and sometimes for higher levels of compensation are assessed through National Board Certification or a similar assessment. Massachusetts, Ohio, and Washington are among the states that have created plans for a continuum of performance assessments to guide the teaching career.

But they are not the first to do so. In 2003, New Mexico created a three-tiered licensure system at the state level, with locally aligned evaluations for on-the-job assessments. Based on a portfolio modeled on that of the National Board, teachers must demonstrate increasing competence in order to progress from Provisional Teacher (Level I: the first 3 years) to Professional Teacher (Level II) to Master Teacher (Level III). Each level is accompanied by increased compensation and responsibilities.[19]

This has created an aligned system that focuses teachers on what their students learn as a result of their teaching decisions, and on how they can learn to improve their effectiveness. Teachers feel they are learning as they both develop their own portfolios and score those of other teachers when they are part of the state scoring team. They also learn as they get feedback on their work from colleagues, made more useful by the common language teachers are developing around their practice. And because yearly district evaluations are based on the same standards as the licensing assessments, teachers can continue to work on their practice in a coherent way throughout their careers.

> **An aligned system focuses teachers on what their students learn as a result of their teaching decisions, and on how they can learn to improve.**

In the authorizing legislation, HB212, legislators recognized the need for New Mexico to develop a high-quality teaching force, stating:

Unless the state and school districts find ways to mentor beginning teachers, intervene with teachers while they still show promise, improve the job satisfaction of quality teachers and elevate the teaching profession by shifting to a professional educator licensing and salary system, public schools will be unable to recruit and retain the highest quality teachers in the teaching profession in New Mexico.

To advance from one licensure level to the next, teachers complete a Professional Development Dossier that provides evidence of performance along three dimensions: instruction, student learning, and professional learning. The dossier, which is modeled after the National Board Certification portfolio and includes teaching artifacts and samples of student work, is submitted electronically to a state evaluation board. Classroom evidence of student learning is presented by the teacher in relation to specific curriculum goals and instructional processes.

Like the performance-based assessments described earlier, the evaluation of the dossier is conducted by outside evaluators, trained to score reliably. Two certified reviewers, who are master teachers from outside the teacher's district, score the dossier. At least one of them is certified in the submitting teacher's field. Reviewer scores are monitored for consistency by a consulting partner organization, Resources for Learning, which is currently engaged in a joint effort with the University of New Mexico College for Education and the Institute for Professional Development to build an infrastructure for professional development to improve student achievement. Thus, the evaluation system and the professional development system are designed to be mutually reinforcing.

> **Performance indicators at each licensure level span three critical areas—instruction, student learning, and professional learning.**

The performance indicators at each licensure level span three critical areas—instruction, student learning, and professional learning—for each of nine competencies:

1. The teacher accurately demonstrates knowledge of the content area and approved curriculum.

2. The teacher appropriately utilizes a variety of teaching methods and resources for each area taught.
3. The teacher communicates with and obtains feedback from students in a manner that enhances student learning and understanding.
4. The teacher comprehends the principles of student growth, development, and learning, and applies them appropriately.
5. The teacher effectively utilizes student assessment techniques and procedures.
6. The teacher manages the educational setting in a manner that promotes positive student behavior and a safe and healthy environment.
7. The teacher recognizes student diversity and creates an atmosphere conducive to the promotion of positive student involvement and self-concept.
8. The teacher demonstrates a willingness to examine and implement change as appropriate.
9. The teacher works productively with colleagues, parents, and community members.

The performance expectations (indicators) describe the observable teacher behaviors required for a teacher to "Meet Expectations" for the competency area, and these indicators become more challenging at higher levels. For example, as shown in the accompanying box, the standards for the first competency area—knowledge of the content area and approved curriculum—anticipate that Level I teachers will use the state standards for planning, will demonstrate content knowledge, and will be clear in their communications with students. At Level II, teachers are further expected to make the curriculum relevant to students, recognize when students need further clarification, address specific learning needs and prior knowledge, and integrate other disciplines into the curriculum. At Level III, teachers use their extensive content and pedagogical knowledge not only to address students' learning needs and prior knowledge, but also to anticipate potential misunderstandings. They both make the content relevant and make connections across lessons and subject areas.[20]

NEW MEXICO COMPETENCIES AT LEVELS I, II, AND III

Competency I. The teacher accurately demonstrates knowledge of the content area and approved curriculum

Competent Level I: Teachers use the state standards and the approved curriculum as the basis of instructional planning. In classroom instruction, they communicate content knowledge, learning goals, directions, and procedures. In communication and interactions related to content, their spoken language is clear and standard, and written language is legible. They use vocabulary correctly for the content and the age of students. They are able to display content knowledge to students and make connections to other disciplines.

Competent Level II: Teachers expand on the state standards and the approved curriculum to make them more relevant for students. During instructional activities, they clearly communicate content knowledge, learning goals, directions, and procedures accurately and in substantive detail. Their vocabulary and written language are clear and at an appropriate level. They recognize when students are confused about directions or performance criteria, and they clarify their communication accordingly. On the whole, competent Level II teachers' representations of content are suitable for their students' learning needs and provide students with connections to their prior knowledge and experiences. These teachers display solid content knowledge and finds ways to integrate other disciplines into the curriculum when appropriate.

Competent Level III: Teachers actively build on the state standards and the approved curriculum by providing instruction based on students' prior knowledge and experiences and by anticipating possible student misunderstanding. Directions and procedures are clear. Learning goals are explicit. These teachers' written and spoken vocabulary enriches the lesson. In delivering the curriculum, competent Level III teachers not only display extensive content knowledge and make connections to other disciplines, but they also convey explicit connections to previous lessons and/or other subjects.

This information is excerpted from New Mexico's 3-Tiered Licensure Performance Evaluation Handbook, Third Edition, 2005, which is a copyright-free document published by the New Mexico Public Education Department. Cited with permission.

The decision to advance a teacher from one licensure level to another is based on both the dossier assessment and the school district's recommendation for advancement. The district recommendation relies in large measure on the running records of performance

> **The decision to advance a teacher from one licensure level to another is based on both the dossier assessment and the school district's recommendation.**

that are kept as part of a teacher's annual Professional Development Plan.

Local Teacher Evaluations

The local teacher evaluation process is aligned with the state licensure system. New Mexico defines the following purposes for teacher evaluation: to assist in identifying and building upon teachers' strengths; to serve as the basis for the improvement of instruction; to enhance the implementation of programs and curriculum; to address accountability and teacher quality; and to support fair, valid, and legal decisions for rehire, promotion, or termination.

Both districts and teachers must create Professional Development Plans. Districts must develop a written teacher performance evaluation plan that meets state requirements, including evaluation instruments that measure performance against the standards, a system for data collection that includes classroom observations, a process for providing feedback, and training for teachers and administrators. Classroom observations may be supplemented by videotapes, written documentation of activities, portfolios, reflective journals, and instructional artifacts.

Ongoing, formative evaluation records are kept over the three-year Level I licensure period that precedes tenure and the Level II professional license. The documentation consists of a running record of authentic information about a teacher's performance in the areas of instruction, student learning, and professional learning.

The teacher's Professional Development Plan (PDP) is filed at the beginning of each school year. The teacher and principal establish measureable objectives for the nine teacher competencies. Together they develop a written plan that articulates goals (including the competencies and indicators to be addressed), an action plan, observable results, and a written reflection of the PDP (including an analysis of student achievement and learning growth). The principal observes the teacher during the year and the teacher collects evidence of accomplishment of the objectives. Before the end of the school year, the teacher and the principal meet to assess how well the PDP was carried out and the extent to which measurable objectives were achieved. This sets the stage for next year's goals and for a process of continual improvement.

How the Process Can Improve Teacher and Student Learning

South Valley Academy, a New Mexico school in a low-income rural community, has recently begun to use the PDP process to foster teacher-conducted action research that is focused on measurable goals for student learning. As they undertook to strengthen their school's evaluation system to better meet the standards intended by the state, head teacher Julie Radoslovich and consultant Shelley Roberts introduced a process of identifying measurable student learning gains for goals important to the teachers and conducting action research to collect data throughout the year regarding those goals.[21] As a National Board certified teacher herself, Julie understood how valuable it can be to look at student learning as a lens on improving practice.

In the course of this work, Julie noted that the state's tiered licensure process appears to have strengthened preparation for newer teachers, as they seem to be increasingly comfortable with developing evidence about their instruction, student learning, and professional learning—a process they have had to complete in order to receive their initial licenses (Level I). Furthermore, Julie and her staff found that, "Through our PDP process, teachers and the Head Teacher naturally build evidence the state requires."

The local PDP process can be traced through the experience of Andres Plaza, a beginning science teacher at South Valley Academy, who decided to focus on vocabulary instruction in his chemistry class. In his *rationale*, he described the frustration students experience with chemistry vocabulary:

> Stoichiometry, huh?? Titration, what?? Sodium hypochlorite, who?? Chemistry is more than just learning about the interactions of matter. Chemistry is like learning another language: a language that codes for complex interactions and physical phenomenon. And, if Chemistry is

studied without an understanding and use of this other language, it is as if you are speaking Spanish to a Brazilian. It doesn't make much sense. Thus, when I reflect about how I can enhance learning in Chemistry, I remember that I am teaching more than a content area; I am teaching a new language.

Andres' goal in 2011–2012 was for 80% of his students to learn the vocabulary necessary for understanding *every* content-related targeted skill. The previous year only 58% of his students learned all of the content vocabulary necessary to demonstrate such proficiency in lab reports. Andres brainstormed with colleagues from various departments: how they develop vocabulary, book titles about building vocabulary, who to observe teaching vocabulary. His PDP action steps included trying out a variety of strategies: PowerPoint presentations, hands-on activities, two-column notes, flashcards, word walls, art posters, and games (e.g., "Around the World," "Mile a Minute"). Afterward, he surveyed students about their favorite strategies for learning vocabulary, while collecting data about students' vocabulary skills scores in each content area.

During the year, the staff collaborate on their PDP activities: giving and receiving peer feedback about measurable goals, resources, action steps, and artifacts to collect; offering advice about students, strategies, and the interpretation of data. Andres said,

> These collaborations are perhaps the most powerful and useful part of the PDP process. Staff became aware of the many learning gaps that we are noticing in our students, and we began working collaboratively to share and find ways to address those learning gaps. Many times other staff members noticed things that were happening that I hadn't noticed before, but as soon as they said it, I was like, "Yeah, that's happening with my students, too." In many of the meetings, teachers together can start noticing trends, and then the project is even more meaningful. I think the PDP process has organically led some of us to addressing skill gaps that might not just be content specific, but to overall academic skill deficits specifically in regards to our school. Having a forum to share effective strategies for student learning opens the door for every teacher at the school to help every other teacher get better. When other people start doing new things because of other people's PDPs, this makes the process even more powerful.

Andres's final reflection included data showing the distribution of vocabulary mastery scores for each content area, allowing him to see which skills were mastered and which needed more work. He also included an analysis of the vocabulary strategies he implemented, and 14 artifacts: sample PowerPoint presentations, word walls, art posters, lab reports, and tests. His final reflection touched on his past, present, and future PDP experiences:

> My PDP for the 2011–2012 school year was the most challenging in my three years at South Valley Academy. During the past two years, I have selected topics that I was an expert in and focused on effective instruction of those topics. In my first year, I focused on how to communicate and use data in scientific writing, and last year on how to use technology tools to improve the depth of data analysis. However, this year I focused on vocabulary instruction, something I never really had to worry about in my own education as well as a topic I have little formal training on how to instruct. At the end of this year of experimentation, I may not have skillfully executed the instructional techniques I was trying to learn, but I learned some big lessons about effective teaching strategies, and even bigger global lessons about how students learn and acquire vocabulary. I look forward to next year when I can continue to focus on vocabulary instruction and a data-based approach to improving those skills with which students struggled.

Having teachers planning their continued growth and targeting new areas in which to promote student learning is exactly what an effective evaluation system should accomplish. Julie concludes:

We can document yearly progress systematically with diverse evidence from multiple sources.

Having experimented with our PDP process these past three years, we find that our practitioner action research evaluation model . . . helps teachers to improve through a culture of feedback. While nurturing teacher performance, we can document yearly progress systematically with diverse evidence from multiple sources. With a fair, transparent process, we can assess teacher quality effectively by using evidence of student learning generated in classrooms.

4   Build Standards-Based Systems of Local Evaluation

I am fortunate to work in a district where the evaluation process is more than a drive-by observation that generates a bunch of paperwork that is a burden to all involved. Instead I am given an opportunity to reflect on my practice, collaborate with my colleagues in a meaningful way, and improve the learning of my students. That's what it's all about.[1]

—Lynn Formigli, National Board Certified Science Teacher,
Santa Clara Unified School District, California

As we saw in Chapter 3, if local school districts' teacher evaluation systems are grounded in the same standards as state licensing and certification systems, and conceptualized as a continuum of assessment and development, they can jointly reinforce teacher learning and growth. The evaluation process at South Valley Academy, embedded in New Mexico's three-tier licensing system, illustrates a productive approach that rests on three components:

> Local evaluation systems grounded in the same standards as state licensing and certification systems, and conceptualized as a continuum, can jointly reinforce teacher learning and growth.

1. **Standards-based evaluations of practice.** Grounded in research-based standards describing effective practice, like those developed by INTASC and adopted by most states, evaluations include observations or videotapes of classroom practice, as well as evidence of teachers' plans, assignments, and student work samples.
2. **Evidence of teacher's contributions to student learning.** Such evidence should be evaluated using multiple sources of information from classroom assessments and documentation, student work samples, and—where these are valid

and appropriate for the curriculum and for the students being taught—other school, district, state, or national tests.

3. **Evidence of teachers' contributions to the work of their colleagues and the school as a whole.** Because student learning gains are a function of teachers' collective efforts, evaluations should include evidence about teachers' work with colleagues, parents, and students to advance student success; contributions to curriculum development and school improvement initiatives; and engagement in broader professional learning.

As the evaluation process at South Valley Academy shows, these three factors should be considered in relation to one another and in relation to the teaching context, rather than in isolation. As I discuss in Chapter 5, an integrated approach is necessary to understand how these interdependent factors affect one another and to inform teaching in intelligent ways. As suggested

> **Observation of practice, evidence of student learning, and evidence of professional contributions represent a three-cornered stool.**

Figure 4.1: Teacher and Administrator Evaluation Framework

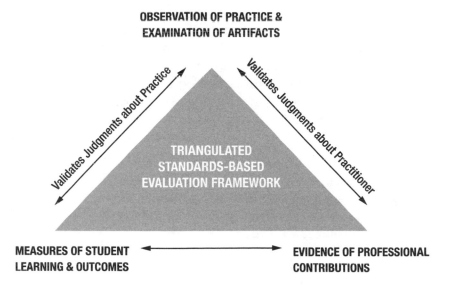

by the Teacher and Administrator Evaluation Framework developed by the Massachusetts Teachers Association (Figure 4.1),[2] observation of practice, evidence of student learning, and evidence of professional contributions represent a three-cornered stool on which the process of teacher development rests.

In this chapter I discuss how the three components of this framework can operate in productive evaluation systems. Because of the intense interest in using student test scores for teacher evaluation—in particular, gains measured by value-added methods—I address the possibilities and pitfalls of these measures more fully in Chapter 5.

STANDARDS-BASED EVALUATIONS OF PRACTICE

Standards-based evaluations of practice are generally guided by systematic observation protocols that provide indicators of teaching effectiveness associated with a set of professional standards. As seen in the example from San Mateo Union High School District in California (see the box on pp. 54–55), the standards describe practices shown by research to be associated with student learning, and they are concrete enough to guide observations and feedback to teachers. The protocols examine teaching along a number of dimensions, such as classroom management, curriculum planning, content knowledge and pedagogy, assessing student learning, and differentiating instruction to meet student needs. Some, like San Mateo's, also include other forms of evidence about practice, such as curriculum units and lesson plans, examples of student assignments, and samples of student work with teacher feedback.

These protocols differ from open-ended forms that allow evaluators to determine, idiosyncratically, what they think is important in the classroom. They also differ from old-style behaviorist approaches that list discrete teaching behaviors that may or may not support learning, such as: "bulletin boards are neat," "teacher keeps a brisk pace of instruction," "objectives are on the board," and so on.

> **Research has found that the frequent, skilled use of standards-based observation with feedback to the teacher is significantly related to student achievement gains.**

Research has found that the frequent, skilled use of standards-based observation with feedback to the teacher is significantly related to student achievement gains, as the process helps teachers improve their practice and effectiveness.[3] Such evaluations are very much like the teacher performance assessments described earlier, as they are based on assessment of practice in light of well-specified teaching standards, except that they occur in real time in the classroom.

> **Ratings determine the intensity of future follow-up.**

In San Mateo, all teachers receive ongoing feedback in light of the standards. Teachers set goals each year in relation to specific standards and identify evidence that can be used to evaluate progress toward the goals. Ratings determine the intensity of future follow-up. A teacher with more than two unsatisfactory ratings enters the Peer Assistance and Review program (further discussed in Chapter 6) and receives intensive mentoring and ongoing evaluation from an expert teacher. Before the year is out, a decision is made by a panel comprised of both teachers and administrators regarding continuation or dismissal.

Greg Jouriles, a teacher at Hillsdale High School in San Mateo, notes that the change to a standards-based system made teacher evaluation much more meaningful for teachers like himself:

> To me, evaluations before [this] system were absolutely meaningless. It was like a one- or two-shot deal. There was no standard to base it on. There was no sense of growth. So one of the things that I like about our new system, especially as a veteran, is that you can pick standards that you want to focus on. You can say, "I want to work on this. This is something that has been bothering me or something that I want to learn more about." I like that ability to self-evaluate and think about what you want to work on. So this year, I am working on graduate profile rubrics [part of the school's project to graduate students based on performance assessments] and that's one of the focuses in my evaluation. And there's a particular content area that I want to focus on—and that's standard three. . . . I think using the CSTPs [California Standards for the Teaching Profession] has been great. Because if you look at those standards. . . I mean, if I could do all of those things I'd be great! It's daunting. But it's given people a better sense of what teaching is in a broader sense.

STANDARDS-BASED EVALUATION
IN SAN MATEO, CALIFORNIA

The California Standards for the Teaching Profession guide teacher licensing in California as well as evaluation systems in many local districts. The standards address the following areas:

1. Engaging and supporting all students in learning
2. Creating and maintaining effective environments for student learning
3. Understanding and organizing subject matter for student learning
4. Planning instruction and designing learning experiences for all students
5. Assessing student learning
6. Developing as a professional educator

Each standard contains five subcategories. In San Mateo, these are rated using a rubric with levels from unsatisfactory to exemplary, based on both supervisors' observations and collection of evidence about each of the standards. To supplement what is observed by the evaluator about a specific standard, teachers are invited to include evidence from their lesson plans, assignments, samples of student work, test scores and other evidence of student learning, student self-assessments, student or parent communications or evaluations, and/or videotapes of classroom practice.[4] An example from the first standard follows:

I. Engaging and Supporting All Students in Learning

Element	Unsatisfactory	Satisfactory	Accomplished	Exemplary
1.1 The teacher builds on the students' prior knowledge, life experiences, and interests to achieve learning goals.	Makes limited connections between the learning goals and students' prior knowledge, life experiences, and interests. Does not encourage student questions or comments during a lesson.	Makes acceptable connections between the learning goals and students' prior knowledge, life experiences, and interests. Elicits some questions from students during a lesson to monitor student understanding.	Makes substantial connections between the learning goals and students' prior knowledge, life experiences, and interests. Elicits and uses questions and comments from students during a lesson to extend their understanding.	Employs strategies that allow all students to connect and apply their prior knowledge, life experiences, and interests to new learning and the achievement of learning goals. Builds on students' questions and comments during lessons to modify instruction.

Element	Unsatisfactory	Satisfactory	Accomplished	Exemplary
1.2 The teacher uses a variety of instructional strategies and resources that respond to students' diverse needs.	Uses limited instructional strategies, and they lack variety, are poorly carried out, or are inappropriate to the students or to the instructional goals. Few adjustments are made to respond to students' needs.	Uses a selection of instructional strategies that are largely appropriate to the students and the instructional goals. They may lack variety or be less than responsive to students' needs.	Uses a variety of instructional strategies that are appropriate to the students and the instructional goals. The teacher carries out these strategies thoughtfully, making some adjustments that are responsive to students' needs.	Makes skillful use of a wide repertoire of instructional strategies to engage all students in learning, making adjustments while teaching to respond to students' needs.
1.3 The teacher facilitates challenging learning experiences for all students in environments that promote autonomy, interaction, and choice.	Directs most learning experiences, permitting limited autonomy, interaction, or choice.	Directs some learning experiences, and permits some autonomy, interaction, and choice.	Facilitates learning experiences to promote autonomy, interaction, and choice, and to encourage and support student involvement in learning.	Provides opportunities for students to collaborate in a variety of constructive interactions; provides environments that promote autonomy and choice in the pursuit of significant learning.

Jouriles also noted that revising the evaluation system was an opportunity to create more coherence across the parts of the system, as well as across the continuum from student teaching to beginning teaching to ongoing development:

> We realized you had to change the culture and that evaluation should be part of professional development. This was happening when Peer

Assistance and Review legislation was coming through and [the new teacher induction program] was being implemented, so we realized that if we tied what we were doing with evaluation to [these programs] we could potentially have a system with common language, common standards, and we could connect the evaluation to professional development.

It's a good design, it's connected to what student teachers are getting [in their preservice teacher education program] because it's connected to the standards, it's about having a portfolio, and it's about self-reflection, about looking for areas of growth.

New teachers at Hillsdale confirm that the system continues and reinforces their learning from their preparation program. English teacher Sarah Press remarks:

The CSTPs were part of our teacher training at STEP [Stanford Teacher Education Program] and part of the rubric for evaluation at Hillsdale so they are something we know and understand and are really comfortable with. They are important touchstones in the profession. We've used them for so long that they are intrinsic and we can really start to see growth within our own practice based on the standards.

> **In standards-based evaluation systems, researchers found that teachers' ratings were related to effectiveness with students, and teachers' effectiveness improved as they worked within the system.**

In a study of three districts using standards-based evaluation systems, researchers found that teachers' ratings were related to their effectiveness with students, and that teachers' effectiveness improved as they worked within the system, receiving ongoing feedback.[5] In the schools and districts studied, formative and summative assessments of teachers were based on well-articulated standards of practice assessed through frequent observations of teaching conducted by expert evaluators, pre- and postobservation interviews, and, sometimes, artifacts such as lesson plans, assignments, and samples of student work.

At Hillsdale, it is easy to see how the process, when well implemented, results in teacher learning. Jeff Gilbert, principal of one of the school's three small learning communities, describes how the system operates:

> The best thing the team did [in creating this system] was to be really clear on the standards that we look at. They are based on the CSTPs and the rubrics are both broad enough to hit on the most important work that teachers do and very specific. They were turned into fairly accessible rubrics that begin the entire process. Teachers are evaluated formally in their first two years in the district and then, if they meet the standard, we expect they then rotate into an "expedited" evaluation, using the same standards and rubrics. The fourth year out they do another full evaluation so then there's a pattern of full, expedited, full, expedited, full.
>
> [As administrators], we can suggest one of the two standards that they are going to focus on. Of the 6 standards the 6th one—professional responsibility—is automatic. [We always ask] what are you doing in terms of your professional development and your participation in the community? Then, they choose two more. I usually coach them regarding which of these standards would work best. So for example, one of the new teachers just had an evaluation conference, and I guided her to the *student engagement* and *instructional practice* standards, because I felt like those two would have the most impact on her performance. We talked through it, and she agreed that those are good to focus on. With more experienced teachers, they'll usually come in and say, "hey, I really want to focus on this standard," and that's fine.
>
> [Teachers] do a self-evaluation, that's the first step of the process. And they use the rubrics and mark them up, and then they write about their strengths and weaknesses within the criteria and they send that to me. This year for the first time, almost half of the teachers are doing googledocs, so as they share them with me I am making comments and they comment back, so we are actually co-creating the self-evaluation document. In fact, as I sit in a class, I'll usually use some of their own language in some of my questions, then I'll type that into the googledoc as an italicized question and they can respond in real time about why they choose to do this or what they will do if students don't understand that. So this is a living document; the self-evaluation document becomes the foundation for feedback along the way throughout the year.

I do walk-throughs every two weeks for the teachers. So by the time we get to the formal evaluation in October or November, I've already been in their classrooms about 4 times. That means that there is very little that's surprising. I don't walk in and that's my first time in there. It lowers the anxiety for both the students and the teacher. One memorable line from my administrator credential program was that, "when you're the evaluator doing an evaluation, for you, it's just another dance. For the teacher, it's the prom." There is anxiety; it's an evaluation. So the more I can be "hey, I'm just dropping in—I was here last week, but this is going to be a little bit longer," the better.

The first formal evaluation involves a full class period and a full hour debrief afterwards. I share what I saw and we talk about their self-evaluation—you know, what did they see themselves—and then we try and reshape the assessment document. In the formal evaluation, I include all of what I see in the walk-throughs in my write-up. So it's all valid and cumulative. We don't want to put on the show; we don't just want to see them at their best. If I go in 15 times over the course of the year, I am going see them at their best and I'm going to see them when they are struggling. And that's when we are going to be able to help them grow.

Teachers say they find this approach to evaluation to be valuable. They feel supported in their learning by both their principal and colleagues. As Sarah Press put it:

We need evaluation as teachers in order to push our thinking forward; there is value in that. . . . It's part of being an educator—we need to know what we can do better. The way it's set up here is that instead of hiding what we are struggling with, we are like: "Please come in here and watch this class. I'm really struggling and I could use your feedback." Evaluation here is a means of praise and improvement—we talk about what went well and what could improve. We have a different attitude about failure in general.

Her colleague, Karl Lindgren-Streicher, a beginning social studies teacher from the same teacher education program, reaffirms this view:

Here I have a lot of confidence as a teacher because I can take risks. There is a lot of trust. I have the leeway to make changes and adjustments based on what I think will work best for the kids. I can bounce an idea off of my principal and she will tell me to run with it. And she will check in on me and be that sounding board. . . . I almost want to bomb a lesson so that I can dissect it and pull it apart and see what I did wrong, what I can do better the next time. It sounds crazy but it's true.

Both Sarah and Karl also underscore the fact that the faculty of the school works as a collegial team to strengthen their individual and collective practice. Because standard 6—*developing as a professional educator*—is always a required goal, this is a fundamental value of the school and the evaluation system. This standard calls on teachers to reflect on their practice and actively engage in professional learning, learn about and work with local communities to meet students' needs, and work proactively with school colleagues to improve school quality.

At Hillsdale, teachers work as members of grade-level teams within small learning communities and share planning time to talk about both their curriculum plans and their students' individual needs. A collaborative commitment is part of the hiring process and is a touchpoint for evaluation. As Sarah explains:

It starts with the interview process. If someone isn't in the mindset and aligned to our culture of collaboration and improvement, then it isn't a fit. There have been people who didn't fit, and they somehow decided to leave on their own. You don't want to be the one that stands out in that way. Also, we are given the time to become better teachers, we have teams that we work with constantly. . . . At Hillsdale the importance of being a good teacher is systemic—we hold each other accountable—we are open to change if something is not working and that's the thing that drives the evaluation system. No one wants to be the teacher who is not getting results, who is not making students think, who is not continuously improving.

PROFESSIONAL CONTRIBUTIONS

As these comments suggest, in a school that is a learning organization, it is as important to be committed to the learning and improvement of the whole school as it is to be committed to one's own development. Thus, another leg of the three-legged stool is teachers' involvement in the general improvement of instruction in the school.

The Importance of Collaborative Work

Collaboration among educators is critical, not just because working with other teachers is a nice thing to do and makes school a more pleasant place to be. In fact, it turns out that high-performing schools—like high-performing businesses—organize people to take advantage of each other's knowledge and skills, so that the whole is far greater than the sum of the parts.

In one recent study, economists were able to quantify the student learning gains generated by the collective expertise of teams of teachers. They found that most value-added gains were attributable to teachers who were more experienced and better qualified, and who stayed together as teams within their schools. The researchers found that peer learning among small groups of teachers was the most powerful predictor of improved student achievement over time.[6] Another recent study found that students achieved more in mathematics and reading when they attended schools characterized by higher levels of teacher collaboration for school improvement.[7] No doubt this is because the teachers built a more coherent curriculum and set of practices across the department or school, and because they could share strategies and insights to help one another improve.

> **Peer learning among small groups of teachers was the most powerful predictor of improved student achievement over time.**

It is not surprising, then, that over 90% of the nation's teachers report that their colleagues contribute to their teaching effectiveness.[8] Contrary to the factory model system designed for isolated teachers to work alone at different spots on the assembly line, education is a team sport. Successful schools raise achievement because they assemble the right mix of skills and abilities, and enable people to work collaboratively.

As a consequence, it is important that evaluation systems take into account the ways in which teachers may support their colleagues and the work of the school. These contributions could include developing and sharing curriculum; supporting colleagues through peer observations, mentoring, or coaching; taking leadership roles in school-improvement initiatives; engaging in outreach to parents; and a variety of other activities that enable the school team to become more effective. In Singapore and many other countries, these collegial activities are weighted heavily in teacher evaluation, and are taken as a sign of leadership that can place a teacher on one of several paths on the career ladder.[9]

> **It is important that evaluation systems take into account ways in which teachers support their colleagues and the work of the school.**

Recognizing and Assessing Contributions to School-Wide Goals

Teachers' contributions to the work of the school as a whole can include specific kinds of *knowledge and skills*, engagement in *shared instructional practices* or *specific student supports*, and support for *collegial learning and school improvement*.

Knowledge and Skills. Schools need a mix of knowledge, skills, and abilities among their faculties to inform curriculum decisions and to meet the needs of their students. Aside from the knowledge of content and pedagogy that teachers generally acquire in their certification area, specialized knowledge about the teaching of English language learners or the teaching of special education students may be highly desirable. Knowledge of the home languages students speak is also essential for communicating with parents as well as students, and is especially useful when it allows teachers to engage children and families and help their colleagues do so. Proficiency in using specific educational techniques, such as Reading Recovery or inquiry-based science, may be important in certain contexts, as it supports both students and colleagues in expanding their success.

> Efforts to evaluate and compensate teachers based directly on students' test scores can create unintended dysfunctional consequences.

Recognizing teachers' knowledge and skills stands in contrast to efforts to evaluate and compensate teachers based directly on students' test scores, which can create a number of unintended dysfunctional consequences, as we describe in the next section. Odden and colleagues note:

> Knowledge- and skills-based compensation systems provide a mechanism to link pay to the knowledge and skills (and by extension, performance) desired of teachers. . . . The concept of knowledge- and skills-based pay in education was adapted from the private sector, where it was developed to encourage workers to acquire new, more complex, or employer-specific skills. Knowledge- and skills-based pay was also intended to reinforce an organizational culture that values employee growth and development and to create a clear career path linked to increasing professional competence.[10]

Odden and colleagues offer several examples of knowledge- and skills-based evaluation and compensation plans.[11] For example:

- Coventry, Rhode Island, provides stipends for National Board Certification and for teachers to develop their skills in authentic pedagogy, self-reflection, differentiated instruction, and family and community involvement—all strategies that have been linked through research to student achievement.
- Douglas County, Colorado, offers compensation for completing blocks of courses associated with district goals, such as student assessment or teaching diverse learners.
- Vaughan Learning Center, a charter school in Los Angeles, California, offers compensation for relevant degrees and certification, as well as for specific knowledge and skills relevant to the school's mission, such as literacy training, training for teaching English as a second language, training

for the inclusion of special education students, and technology training.

Shared Instructional Practices. As schools seek to offer a more coherent approach to instruction, they need to encourage teachers to share practices, especially those that have a positive impact on student achievement. For example, the use of formative assessment to provide feedback to students and the provision of opportunities for them to revise their work have been found in many dozens of studies to greatly increase student learning gains.[12] Teachers who teach students specific metacognitive strategies for reading, writing, and mathematical problem solving have been found to produce increased student learning of complex skills.[13] In addition, teachers who have developed specific skills for teaching English language learners are more successful with these students.[14]

> Schools need to encourage teachers to share practices, especially those that have a positive impact on student achievement.

In some systems, teachers receive recognition for demonstrating that they have implemented particular new practices associated with school-wide or district-wide goals, such as the use of common literacy practices across classrooms, the use of formative assessments in planning and modifying instruction, or the implementation of a new system of writing instruction. Where possible, these practices are documented, along with evidence of how the changes have affected student participation and learning, thus tying professional contribution directly to student learning. In addition to specific teaching practices, a teacher might document how she increased student attendance or homework completion through regular parent conferences and calls home. She might show evidence of changes in these student outcomes, as well as outcomes such as improved grades or stronger graduation rates. The rationale for using these measures of effective teaching practices is that they support teacher development and improve the conditions for student learning.

Support for Collegial Learning and School Improvement. In the earlier examples from Hillsdale High School, we saw how teachers function as part of a team and as members of a collegial faculty continually striving to improve learning for all of their students. Systems are set up so that teachers have built-in collaboration time to discuss curriculum and student concerns within their grade-level teams in each of the houses (e.g., small learning communities serving about 400 students each). At a recent team meeting, for example, teachers talked about:

- student grades and how to help students improve,
- specific students' academic performance and behavioral issues,
- upcoming units, including cross-curricular units,
- how to infuse advisory topics (such as building a growth mind-set in students) into everyday classroom activities,
- study tips, such as an iPhone app that allows students to make flashcards on their phones or computers and share with others in the class as a study tool,
- finding incentives for students who are underperforming in one class but not in another,
- how to support study hall for some students who struggle with staying after school,
- grade verification sheets, and
- homework and upcoming projects.

In this context, teachers' participation in the joint efforts of the team—including learning from the experience of colleagues and engaging in the necessary follow-up for plans to be implemented collectively—is a clear expectation. The evaluation process can record evidence of both this participation and follow-through, as well as a willingness to learn from others and contribute to their success.

It is also possible to formalize the work of teaching teams in the evaluation process. For example, in Rochester, New York, teachers in good standing can choose to be evaluated through a collegial system called the Performance Appraisal Review for Teachers (PART). Negotiated in Rochester in 1987, PART allows self-selected groups of teachers, in the same school or across schools, to design an annual or multiyear project related to improved teaching and learning, set goals for themselves, and then be evaluated not just as individual practitioners but also as members of a teaching team. This promotes teacher collaboration and contextualizes teacher assessment within the reality of teachers' day-to-day actual work. PART has also promoted innovation, interdisciplinary approaches, project-based learning, and performance-based assessments, moving the collective practice of teaching forward.[15]

EVIDENCE OF STUDENT LEARNING

The third critical leg of the three-legged stool is evidence of student learning. It is important to look at student learning in connection to teaching in the course of the evaluation process. There are many ways to do this—from systematic collection of evidence about student learning gains, as I describe further in the next chapter, to incorporating work aimed at improving student learning as an organic part of a teacher development process. This latter approach is the strategy currently in focus at Hillsdale High in San Mateo, and it contributes to teachers' strong sense that they are supported in multiple ways to improve their practice. Principal Jeff Gilbert describes the school's current work on this aspect of evaluation:

> Student work and evidence . . . is a focus both at the district level and for me here at the site. The system was set up so that teachers would do a portfolio around their two standards. So if they picked assessment as one of their standards they would collect assessments and present them to me. What we have been pushing on here at Hillsdale is how to focus in on very specific teaching events, moments, and student work that the teacher and I will sit down and analyze together. We use a variety of strategies to improve student learning.
>
> For example, let's say I learn after the first observation that a teacher is worried about the performance of a particular cohort of students in chemistry and concerned they might fail the class: Our action plan is for

me to do a focus group with those students and talk to them and take notes. I'll tell the kids, "We want to get information from you about what's working and what's not, what helps you succeed and what doesn't," and then sit down with the teacher, because this is aligned to her evaluation goal, and debrief the focus group. From there, we will create some steps that will lead to changing her practice. So instead of her getting lots of stuff [in a portfolio] and showing off to me, in an hour we can do this more focused conversation, and that can be a follow-up to the debrief meeting.

As another example, we have a teacher working on standard five, assessment, so she is collecting all her assessments, formal and informal, on her unit on *Lord of the Flies*. Then we are going to sit down and look at those, and I am going to reflect to her and say: "This is what I'm seeing in this assessment. It seems like you are measuring this. Was that your intention?" In our initial conference, she looked at a few questions she had asked and then, as we talked, she came to the conclusion that, if she was measuring on a rubric, she wasn't being clear enough to the students about what it would take to move to the highest level of the rubric. So students were stopping before they got there. As a result, she wasn't sure if students were getting what they needed. She determined that, you know, "I think this question is flawed; I don't think I wrote the question well enough to draw out the type of response that I'm looking for, and I'm not sure if they really know this." So that is a great moment and we want to build on that.

Once teachers identify an area they want to work on, they can collect more focused evidence of student learning in relation to the problem they are trying to solve or the area they are seeking to develop. This evidence can be part of the evaluation process throughout the year, as well as at the end of the year, and can be a vehicle for stimulating professional learning of various kinds. The evaluator is a facilitator of this process. As Gilbert indicates:

> **Once teachers identify an area they want to work on, they can collect more focused evidence of student learning.**

I feel like my job in the evaluation process is to present them with some options for their development toward their goals: they could do peer observations; they could do lesson study; they could do an analysis of student work where we bring in the task with samples of high, medium and low [performance] and try to figure out why students are performing at different levels. That to me is the most exciting thing we are doing now—this switch to the more sophisticated way of looking at student outcomes and student work within the evaluation process.

> **Evidence of student learning is combined with other evidence from standards-based teaching evaluations conducted through classroom observation, and evidence of teachers' skills or practices.**

Whereas this kind of work is relatively new in most districts, it has been going on for more than two decades in districts that are part of Arizona's career ladder program. Teachers' goal-setting to guide the collection of learning evidence plays a major role in this program, which has provided state incentives to create innovative evaluation and compensation plans. Participating districts have long used student learning data to ascertain teaching effectiveness. (See box: Use of Student Learning Evidence in Amphitheater, Arizona, which describes one of these districts.) In all of the systems created by local districts, evidence of student learning is combined with other evidence from standards-based teaching evaluations conducted through classroom observation, and evidence of teachers' skills or practices as described earlier.

One study of the Arizona career-ladder programs found that, over time, participating teachers demonstrated an increased ability to:

- create tools to assess student learning gains in their classrooms;
- develop and evaluate pre- and posttests;
- define measurable outcomes in "hard-to-quantify" areas such as art, music, and physical education; and
- monitor student learning growth in relation to their action plans.

They also showed:

- a greater awareness of the importance of sound curriculum development,
- more alignment of curriculum with district objectives, and
- increased focus on higher-quality content, skills, and instructional strategies.[16]

USE OF STUDENT LEARNING EVIDENCE IN AMPHITHEATER, ARIZONA

More than 20 years ago, Arizona created incentives for districts to develop career ladders that base evaluation and advancement in part on evidence of student learning. One of these districts, Amphitheater, structures teachers' analysis of student learning evidence in several ways.

First, teachers set year-long goals for their students based on their initial achievement and state standards. Then, for one or more of these goals, they choose an assessment tool that they can use for a pre-assessment, mid-year assessment, and end-of-year assessment. In their evaluation, teachers provide copies of these assessments and a data sheet that lists outcomes for all of their students on each of these assessments. These data are the basis for further analysis. At the beginning, middle, and end of the year, teachers answer these kinds of questions:

1. Reflect on the student results from your assessment.
   a. Identify and describe the areas of your students' strengths and weaknesses as they pertain to your goals (pre-assessment).
   b. Identify why students regressed, stayed at the same level, and/or grew more than expected (mid- or post-assessment).
2. Looking at the results of students in three groups (high, medium, low), explain the instructional practices you will use to increase the achievement of each group.
3. How will students use assessment results to further their learning (e.g., student goal-setting and reflection, etc.)? Include three (3) student work samples evidencing the 21st-Century Skills explained in the Student Achievement Plan. Submit samples of student work from high-, medium-, and low-quality results with Student Work Sample Cover Sheets.

4. Describe specific actions taken for individual students who are not demonstrating growth, not meeting the growth targets, or exceeding the identified growth targets. **Interventions** are actions taken to individualize learning for students who are not making significant growth. **Extensions** are actions taken for students who have surpassed their growth targets before the end of the year.

These data and reflections on student progress are part of the teacher's portfolio, along with a professional growth plan that outlines activities the teacher plans to pursue, their expected impact on student learning, and sources of evidence for evaluating that impact. In addition, teachers who want to advance on the career ladder must lead and participate in a collaborative action research group. The group explores a topic based on student needs. Teachers individually document the impact of instruction on student achievement.

For more information, see: www.amphi.com/departments—programs/career-ladder/collaborative-action-research-(car)-2011-2012.aspx

Used in this way, student learning evidence incorporated into teacher evaluation can lead to improvements in practice.

There are many productive ways to build a standards-based system that incorporates evidence of practice, student learning, and professional contributions. However, we have also discovered potential pitfalls of efforts to tie student achievement to teacher evaluation in inappropriate ways. I discuss those in the next chapter, along with more useful strategies for connecting teaching, learning, and evaluation.

5 Use Evidence of Student Learning Appropriately

I do what I do every year. I teach the way I teach every year. [My] first year got me pats on the back. [My] second year got me kicked in the backside. And for year three, my scores were off the charts. I got a huge bonus, and now I am in the top quartile of all the English teachers. What did I do differently? I have no clue.[1]

—A Houston teacher commenting on the annual changes in her value-added test scores

Recent emphasis on evaluating teachers by looking at the results of their teaching, as well as what they do, is an important step in the right direction. It is a step that was first taken by the National Board for Professional Teaching Standards two decades ago when it included student learning evidence linked to evidence of teaching in teachers' portfolios. Because student learning is the primary goal of teaching, it appears straightforward that it ought to be taken into account in determining a teacher's competence. Yet how to do so is not so simple. As I describe in this chapter, the currently touted strategy of using value-added methods to calculate student test score gains attached to individual teachers has been found to be far less reliable and accurate than many researchers had hoped and most policymakers have assumed. Other strategies that use multiple sources of evidence about student learning are essential to get a fair gauge on what a teacher has accomplished with his or her students.

> **The strategy of using value-added methods to calculate student test score gains attached to individual teachers has been found to be far less reliable and accurate than many researchers had hoped.**

A true story about a teacher in New York City[2] illustrates the point: In 2011, Carolyn Abbott taught 7th- and 8th-grade students at the Anderson School, a school for gifted students on the upper west side of Manhattan.

In 2010, her 7th graders scored at the 98th percentile on the state math test. When she had these students again in 8th grade, they were studying the Regents Integrated Algebra curriculum that is typically taught in high school. By January, all of Carolyn's honors-class 8th graders had taken and passed the Regents exam for the course, one-third of them with perfect scores. Most New York students who pass the exam with the required score of 65 or higher are 10th graders. Parents' comments about Ms. Abbott are glowing:

> Ms. Abbott is a great teacher.

> Ms. Abbott is my son's teacher, and she has been fabulous. He has never learned more math than he has this year.

> Ms. Abbott is one of my daughter's favorite teachers. She helped my daughter develop a love of math, and the kids really enjoy her class.[3]

Despite this noteworthy success, the positive evaluation from her principal, and the fact that she was beloved by her students and parents, Carolyn Abbott received the worst rating of any 8th-grade math teacher in the city on the Teacher Data Reports—New York City's system for calculating value-added scores on the state tests. Although her students did very well on the state 8th-grade math test on which the rating was based, Carolyn scored at the very bottom in the ranking system, which compares teachers to one another in terms of their students' test score gains. In a sense, she was, as researcher Aaron Pallas noted, "a victim of her own success." Having gotten her students to the 98th percentile in the 7th grade, there was very little room for them to grow. Like other state tests across the country, this one does not measure the material that is taught in future grade levels, and thus cannot measure the actual achievement or gains of students who are learning more advanced material. And because of New York's teacher evaluation system, no other tests or student learning evidence are taken into account in the Teacher Data Reports that are used to rank teachers on their so-called "value-added" scores.

New York City's evaluation system also requires that novice teachers reach a certain level on this metric in order to be considered for tenure, unless a case can be made by the principal and approved by the superintendent to override the numbers. Carolyn's principal told her she would make the strongest case she could, but she could not guarantee the result at the next level up in the bureaucracy. Not willing to participate in this system any longer, Carolyn left teaching to enter a PhD program in mathematics. Students at her school had this to say:

> I always loved Ms. Abbott. She is and was an amazing teacher, and no teacher evaluation will ever change that.

> I am a sixth grader at Anderson, and I have been looking forward to having math class with Ms. Abbott since the fourth grade. . . . She is one of the best math teachers ever, in my opinion, and I would do anything to keep her here at Anderson.

How is it that a system designed to find the teachers who are shirking their duties and failing their students could have results that are so far from accurate? Is Carolyn Abbott's situation just an anomaly? Unfortunately not. News outlets across the country have carried many similar stories about teachers who are clearly enabling significant learning for their students, but who are nonetheless receiving surprisingly low or highly variable ratings based on value-added analyses of their students' scores on state tests.[4]

> **Teachers who are clearly enabling significant learning for their students are nonetheless receiving surprisingly low or highly variable ratings based on value-added analyses.**

There are many reasons for these counterintuitive outcomes. A major reason is that even though statistical models try to control for things like student characteristics, it is impossible to remove the effects of differences in classroom composition from the value-added ratings. The group of students who are in a class turn out to have a major effect on how teachers' ratings change from year to year or from class to class. In addition, there are many home and school influences on student learning beyond an individual teacher: student health, attendance, parent support, class sizes, curriculum materials, instructional specialists, and more. At a time when 1 in

4 U.S. students lives in poverty and a growing share are homeless (as many as 1 in 10 in some school districts), these factors can dramatically affect children's lives in ways that impact their learning.

A third reason, which is obvious in this New York teacher example and many others, is that state tests are poor measures for looking at the growth of students who are either very advanced or far behind their peers. This problem was made worse by No Child Left Behind rules requiring that state tests measure only grade-level standards—which means they do not include items that would measure the knowledge of the large share of students who are already scoring above or below grade level. In testing parlance, this means that the tests have a low ceiling and a high floor. They are also less valid for some classes of students, including many special education students, as well as new immigrants and English learners who are required in many states to take the tests soon after they enter the country, before they speak English. Thus, value-added methods can produce hugely distorted ratings for teachers who have concentrations of these students because of the way that students are assigned and classrooms are tracked.

> **Because state tests have a low ceiling and a high floor, and are less valid for some classes of students, value-added methods can produce hugely distorted ratings.**

Proponents of using these measures in teacher evaluation argue that traditional evaluation practices have failed to distinguish among teachers of varying quality, and that other methods, such as teacher observations, may also be unreliable. And it makes intuitive sense that we should use methods that look at how students are gaining on some measures of achievement to ascertain what teachers are accomplishing. This approach is also attractive because it does not require administrator observation time and training of evaluators to score observation protocols and/or to assess the quality of teacher videotapes, student work, or other artifacts. It promises objectivity and a common yardstick, without having to rely on human effort and judgment.

The promises of efficiency and objectivity are seductive, but they are not a sufficient rationale if it turns out that the measures are not accurate or their use undermines the main objectives of teacher evaluation: developing and retaining excellent teachers, and continually improving teaching and learning.

THE BENEFITS AND CHALLENGES OF LOOKING AT LEARNING THROUGH A VALUE-ADDED LENS

Clearly, this set of problems was not the intent of social scientists who developed value-added models (VAMs) to examine student learning. Methods of measuring student achievement after adjusting for prior achievement and some other student and school characteristics have proved highly valuable in the research literature. These approaches are fairer assessments of school progress and program effects than judgments based on students' test scores at a single point in time or comparisons of student cohorts that involve different students at two points in time. One major criticism of the accountability scheme under No Child Left Behind has been that it looks at point-in-time measures of achievement for different cohorts of students, rather than looking how schools have helped individual students make progress. Looking at student achievement gains is a helpful response to that problem.

Furthermore, large-scale research using these methods has produced hundreds of valuable studies of the effects of curriculum approaches, school interventions, out-of-school conditions, and professional development programs on student achievement gains. I have cited many studies using value-added methods in this book. These include studies examining the effectiveness of National Board Certified teachers and the predictive validity of other teacher performance assessments cited in Chapter 2. Recently, the Measures of Effective Teaching research sponsored by the Gates Foundation has sought to validate a number of teacher observation protocols and student surveys against student learning gains on both traditional tests and tests measuring higher-order skills using value-added methods. (See box: Measures of Effective Teaching.) And I have personally conducted many studies of this kind.

Although there are limitations to all research methods— including the limitations posed by the kinds of tests that are typically used to measure achievement, which are especially narrow in the United States, the value of value-added models for large-scale studies of educational effects is well established.[5]

MEASURES OF EFFECTIVE TEACHING

The Measures of Effective Teaching project examined how well several different instruments for classroom observation were able to capture teaching in terms of their reliability across events and scorers, and in terms of their relationship to measured gains in student learning. One of the important aspects of the study was that it looked not only at state test scores, but also other measures, including an open-ended literacy assessment and an assessment of conceptual understanding in mathematics. In addition, it looked at student reports about teaching practice.

The five different approaches to classroom observation reflect dimensions of teaching that emerge from research and are reflected in standards that describe teaching, such as the protocols discussed in Chapter 4. They include:

- The Framework for Teaching (or FFT), developed by Charlotte Danielson;
- The Classroom Assessment Scoring System (or CLASS), developed by Robert Pianta and colleagues at the University of Virginia;
- The Protocol for Language Arts Teaching Observations (or PLATO), developed by Pamela Grossman at Stanford University;
- Mathematical Quality of Instruction (or MQI), developed by Heather Hill of Harvard University; and
- The UTeach Teacher Observation Protocol (or UTOP), developed by Michael Marder and Candace Walkington at the University of Texas-Austin.

The instruments were used to score videotaped observations of more than 1,000 teachers teaching in grades 4 through 8 in five urban school districts. All five of these instruments were found to be positively related to student achievement gains on both sets of tests, although teachers whose students fared well on one measure were not always the same ones whose students excelled on the other. Interestingly, there was a much stronger association between classroom observation scores and student learning on the open-ended English language arts assessment than on the state tests, suggesting that these more expansive assessments may capture more aspects of students' learning and teachers' teaching than the state tests do.

(Continued)

Student feedback about teachers' practice was collected using the Tripod student perception survey, developed by Ron Ferguson at Harvard University. This measure was also positively related to students' learning gains.

This study demonstrated that it is possible to develop tools for observing teachers—both by skilled evaluators and by students—that are related to teachers' effectiveness. The study also showed that results are sensitive to the test being used, which suggests the importance of multiple measures of student learning. It also showed that the most unreliable means of evaluating teachers was the one that weighted test-score gains, rather than observations, the most heavily.

The problem comes in when value-added methods are used to draw conclusions about an individual teacher's effectiveness based on student test scores attached to that teacher. As economist Doug Harris notes, even when value-added measures are valid *on average* across large numbers of teachers, "[t]hey could still be—and apparently are—invalid for specific subgroups of teachers."[6] He points to research illustrating that typical value-added measures are biased in middle and high school because of student tracking.[7] In addition, Harris notes research documenting the problem illustrated by Carolyn Abbott's case, where many students can score at or near the top score on the test and thus cannot show gains over time. This means that "teachers whose students start off with very high achievement will receive lower performance ratings than they deserve because of the test ceiling.'"[8]

In addition to New York, this problem has been noted in states such as Texas and Louisiana,[9] where it is relatively easy for advanced students to score at the very top of the test. In these states, educators have begun to notice that teachers in schools and classrooms with many high-achieving students are rated "ineffective" on the value-added rankings, even though their students are doing very well. Two such ratings can get a teacher fired in Louisiana, where a teacher of gifted students in a magnet school expressed the views of many such teachers when she said that evaluation worries have "made me consider quitting forever because of an assessment which could eventually label me ineffective and cost me my job."[10]

VAM models assume that tests measure the full range of achievement and that students are randomly assigned to teachers, neither of which is true in the real world. Their use for evaluating the effectiveness of individual teachers also assumes that teachers teach similar students under similar conditions, and that the effects of other teachers, parents, and learning conditions will not affect students' scores. As Harris states, "[t]he assumptions underlying value-added models have also been shown to be false;"[11] This may influence differently-situated teachers in different ways. In general, however, a measure cannot be considered valid if it is heavily influenced by factors that are outside the control of teachers.

> **VAM models assume that tests measure the full range of achievement and that students are randomly assigned to teachers, neither of which is true in the real world.**

HOW VALUE-ADDED ACHIEVEMENT MEASURES OPERATE IN THE REAL WORLD

Even before the many recent studies offering evidence about real-world outcomes began to come in, many researchers offered cautions about basing individual teacher evaluations on annual student test scores. Chief among these are the difficulties in attributing student gains to specific teachers, and challenges in disentangling teacher effects from those of school and home conditions, as well as from other student factors.

> **Even before the many recent studies offering evidence about real-world outcomes, researchers offered cautions about basing individual teacher evaluations on annual student test scores.**

Among these influences on learning are multiple teachers, parents, tutors and out-of-school learning supports, home conditions, and a variety of other school conditions, such as curriculum quality, materials, class sizes, and administrative supports.[12] As Henry Braun, then of the Educational Testing Service, concluded in his primer on value-added models:

> It is always possible to produce estimates of what the model designates as teacher effects. These estimates, however, capture the contributions

of a number of factors, those due to teachers being only one of them. So treating estimated teacher effects as accurate indicators of teacher effectiveness is problematic.[13]

Indeed, the most optimistic estimates conclude that only about 7% to 10% of the overall variation in student achievement can be attributed to a student's individual teachers.[14] The largest influences, typically accounting for about 60% of the variance, are socioeconomic factors associated with individual students and the collective composition of the classroom and school.[15] The remaining variation is either a function of school factors other than the teacher—for example, the influences of specific curricula, the availability of useful learning materials, the time teachers have with students, school organizational conditions, administrative and leadership practices, class sizes, the availability of instructional specialists, and the collective efforts of faculty and parents—or is unexplained.

Although teachers account for more of the year-to-year gain in achievement than they do of overall achievement, there are many other home and school influences on gains that are associated with the student (e.g., health, attendance, home context, learning characteristics) and the school (e.g., colleagues, curriculum, and teaching conditions). In addition, on spring-to-spring measures of achievement such as those offered by most state tests, the summer learning loss that substantially undermines the achievement of lower-income students also reduces their measured learning gains and is misattributed to their next year's teacher.[16]

For these reasons and others, Donald Rubin, a leading statistician in the area of causal inference, concluded after reviewing a range of leading VAM techniques:

> We do not think that their analyses are estimating causal quantities, except under extreme and unrealistic assumptions.[17]

Similarly, Henry Braun stated in his review of research:

> VAM results should not serve as the sole or principal basis for making consequential decisions about teachers. There are many pitfalls to making

causal attributions of teacher effectiveness on the basis of the kinds of data available from typical school districts. We still lack sufficient understanding of how seriously the different technical problems threaten the validity of such interpretations.[18]

And a major report by the RAND Corporation concluded:

> The research base is currently insufficient to support the use of VAM for high-stakes decisions about individual teachers or schools.[19]

Instability of Ratings

Because of the many influences on student learning, studies have found that value-added ratings of teacher effectiveness are highly unstable. One study of five large urban districts, for example, found that among top-ranked teachers (the highest 20%) in one year, only 25% to 35% were similarly ranked a year later, while a comparable proportion had moved to the bottom two quintiles. And among the lowest rated, only about 20% to 30% were similarly ranked a year later, while 25% to 45% moved to the upper tier of the rankings over the course of a year.[20] On average, a teacher who scored an A (in the top quintile) in one year had about a 50% chance of scoring a C, D, or F the next year; and a teacher who scored an F (in the bottom quintile) in the first year had about a 50% chance of scoring an A, B, or C the next year[21] (see Figure 5.1). If value-added ratings were really measuring a teacher's basic competence or effectiveness, such wild swings would not occur.

> **A teacher who scored an A (in the top quintile) in one year had about a 50% chance of scoring a C, D, or F the next year.**

For this reason, the National Research Council's Board on Testing and Assessment concluded that:

> VAM estimates of teacher effectiveness . . . should not be used to make operational decisions because such estimates are far too unstable to be considered fair or reliable.[22]

Figure 5.1: Changes in Teachers' Value-Added Ratings from One Year to the Next

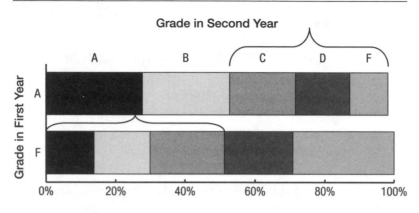

Grades A–F correspond to quintiles 1–5.
Source: Tim Sass (2008).

Bias

If this instability were just "noise," it could be handled by averaging several years of data for teachers, as many proponents of value-added analyses suggest. However, research has found that the test-score gains associated with teachers are affected by differences in the students who are assigned to them, even if those differences are supposed to be "controlled" in the statistical model. In general, except for the special case of highly advanced "gifted" classes in states with low test ceilings, the same teacher appears more effective when he or she is teaching more advantaged students than when he or she is teaching students who experience educational challenges of various kinds. This appears to be especially true for those who have classes with a large number of students who have special education needs or who are new English learners.[23] This is why studies have also found that tracking students into ability groups at the secondary level leads to misestimates of teachers'

> In general, the same teacher appears more effective when he or she is teaching more advantaged students than when teaching students who experience educational challenges.

effectiveness.[24] Tracking is somewhat less common at the elementary level, but it likely has similar effects there as well.

A California study of high school teachers illustrates how these factors operate. The study found that teachers' value-added ratings were significantly related to the percentage of students in their classes from different race/ethnicity, income, language background, and parent education groups, despite the fact that these variables were "controlled" in the statistical models. The correlations between these factors and teachers' value-added ratings ranged from about .3 to .5, depending on the factor and the statistical model used. This means that, from year to year and from class to class, differences in teachers' value-added ratings were associated with differences in the composition of their classes. These correlations are as large as those usually associated with the relationship of teachers' value-added scores from one year to the next. In these data, where teachers had more stable scores, their classes usually had similar student characteristics across years.

As just one example, the rating for an experienced English teacher jumped from the very lowest decile in one year to the very highest decile the next year. Between these two years, the proportion of English learners in her classroom dropped from nearly 60% in year 1 to under 5% in year 2. The proportions of Hispanic and low-income students also decreased, whereas parent education levels increased (see Figure 5.2).

Both this instability of ratings and the ratings' relationship to student characteristics were found in a study in Houston, Texas, where teachers are evaluated for dismissal and merit pay using a value-added system called EVAAS.[25] Houston teachers have come to know that they generally receive lower EVAAS ratings when they are teaching larger numbers of newly mainstreamed English learners. Some highly respected teachers with strong supervisory ratings have been dismissed after taking on such classes in the 4th grade, where students are first transitioned

> **In Houston, highly respected teachers with strong supervisory ratings have been dismissed after taking on classes in the 4th grade, where students are first transitioned into mainstream classes.**

Figure 5.2: Student Characteristics in Two Years for a Teacher Whose Ranking Changed from the 1st to the 10th Decile

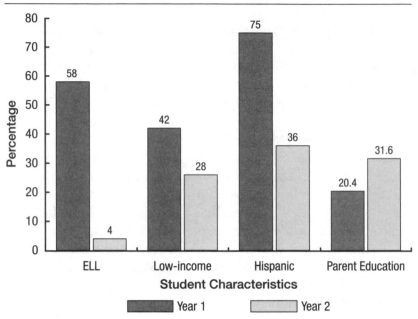

into mainstream classes. One of those dismissed had previously received exemplary ratings from her principal every year and was once voted Teacher of the Year. Her value-added scores, shown in Table 5.1, illustrate both the variability of these ratings from year to year and the effect that teaching a 4th-grade transition class had on her history. It was the effect of that one year's scores, averaged into a 3-year rolling average, that led to her dismissal.

The effect of teaching a class of newly mainstreamed English learners in that 4th-grade transition year is known to Houston teachers. As two teachers commented to researchers:

> I went to a transition classroom, and now there's a red flag next to my name. I guess now I'm an ineffective teacher? I keep getting letters from the district, saying "You've been recognized as an outstanding teacher" . . . this, this, and that. But now because I teach English-language learners who "transition in," my scores drop, and I get a flag next to my name.

I'm scared to teach in the fourth grade. I'm scared I might lose my job if I teach in an [ELL] transition grade level, because I'm scared my scores are going to drop, and I'm going to get fired because there's probably going to be no growth.

Another 4th/5th-grade teacher was adamant: "When they say nobody wants to do 4th grade—nobody wants to do 4th grade! Nobody!" [26]

Similar problems occur for teachers working with large numbers of special education students and with teachers working in gifted and talented programs, where students have already topped out on the test. A teacher of a gifted class explained:

Every year I have the highest test scores, [and] I have fellow teachers that [sic] come up to me when they get their bonuses [based on their EVAAS scores] . . . One recently came up to me [and] literally cried, "I'm so sorry." I'm like, "Don't be sorry . . . It's not your fault." Here I am . . . with the highest test scores and I'm getting $0 in bonuses. It makes no sense year-to-year how this works. . . . You know, I don't know what to do. I don't know how to get higher than a 100%. [27]

The extent to which the composition of the class influences teachers' value-added ratings is also shown by "falsification" studies that test whether the so-called "teacher effect" is really a function of the teacher, or is a function of other variables. These studies look

Table 5.1: EVAAS Scores by Subject, Grade, and Year for One Teacher

EVAAS Scores	2006–2007 Grade 5	2007–2008 Grade 4	2008–2009 Grade 3	2009–2010 Grade 3
Math	− 2.03	+ 0.68*	+ 0.16*	+ 3.46
Reading	− 1.15	− 0.96*	+ 2.03	+ 1.81
Language Arts	+ 1.12	− 0.49*	− 1.77	− 0.20*
Science	+ 2.37	− 3.45	n/a	n/a
Social Studies	+ 0.91*	− 2.39	n/a	n/a
ASPIRE Bonus	$3,400	$700	$3,700	$0

*Scores are not significantly different from the reference gain scores of other teachers across HISD.

Source: Amrein-Beardsley & Collins (2012).

at teachers' "effects" on their students in grade levels *before* or *after* the grade level in which the teacher actually had those students. Logically, for example, a 5th-grade teacher cannot have influenced her students' test scores two years earlier in 3rd grade. So a model that identifies teachers' true effects should show *no* such effect. But studies that have looked at this question have shown large "effects" of a teacher on his or her students in years when he or she did not teach them. This illustrates that other factors associated with that group of students have at least as much bearing on the value-added measure as the teacher who actually taught them in a given year.[28]

Measurement Concerns

Another concern is that teachers' value-added scores also differ significantly when different tests are used, even when these are within the same content area.[29] As economist Jesse Rothstein has noted, for example:

> **Teachers' value-added scores also differ significantly when different tests are used.**

- In a study using two tests measuring basic skills and higher-order skills, 20% to 30% of teachers who ranked in the top quartile in terms of their impacts on state tests ranked in the bottom half of impacts on more conceptually demanding tests (and vice versa).[30]
- Another study found that teachers' estimated effectiveness is very different for different subscales of the same math test (*Procedures*, generally measuring calculation skills, and *Problem Solving*, generally measuring more complex conceptual skills).[31]
- Teachers' measured effects on high-stakes tests are not strongly related to their effects on low-stakes tests, and their effects on high-stakes test scores dissipate more quickly.[32]

Furthermore, concerns have been raised about the narrowness of current, largely multiple-choice, basic skills tests, and the possibility that test-based evaluation will lead to teaching to tests at the expense of other kinds of learning, such as writing, inquiry, and complex problem solving. This fear is reinforced by studies that have found that, under conditions of high-stakes accountability, large majorities of teachers report having changed their instruction to focus on the content and format of state tests, while de-emphasizing subjects and modes of performance that are not on the test.[33] As a Florida teacher observed, even before scores were used for teacher evaluation:

> Before FCAT I was a better teacher. I was exposing my children to a wide range of science and social studies experiences. I taught using themes that really immersed the children into learning about a topic using their reading, writing, math, and technology skills. I know that the way I was teaching was building a better foundation for my kids. Now I'm basically afraid to NOT teach to the test.[34]

And a Texas teacher noted:

> I have seen more students who can pass the [state test] but cannot apply those skills to anything if it's not in that format. I have students who can do the test but can't look up words in a dictionary and understand the different meanings. . . . As for higher quality teaching, I'm not sure I would call it that. Because of the pressure for passing scores, more and more time is spent practicing the test and putting everything in [the test] format.[35]

Incentives

Since the use of test-based teacher evaluation was required by the federal government as part of Race to the Top and as a prerequisite for flexibility waivers under No Child Left Behind, it has become a part of state policy in more than half of the states. Many of them use VAM models for measuring student achievement growth and count the measures for up to 50% of the final evaluation rating. Some require an "effectiveness" rating on this measure as a condition of continuation or tenure, effectively counting it as 100% of the judgment for many teachers. Given the high stakes associated with these measures in many places, it is important to consider the incentives that these measures create for teacher behaviors.

In terms of incentives, proponents hope that evaluating teachers based on their students' scores will focus teachers on raising student scores, and this is certainly likely to happen. At the same time, educators and analysts have raised concerns about the incentives to narrow the curriculum by "teaching to the test" at the expense of other kinds of learning. Analysts have also raised concerns about the possible disincentives for teachers to work together collaboratively in a system that ranks them against one another, along with disincentives for teachers to serve students who do not yet speak English and those who have special education needs, and whose test scores therefore may not accurately reflect their learning. This could inadvertently reinforce current practices in which inexperienced teachers are disproportionately

> **The instability and bias of the measures may cause the wrong teachers to be fired and other capable teachers to quit.**

assigned to the neediest students and schools discourage high-need students from entering or staying.[36] Finally, the instability and bias of the measures may cause the wrong teachers to be fired and other capable teachers to quit the profession altogether. As an Economic Policy Institute report written by a group of noted scholars concludes:

> Basing teacher evaluation primarily on student test scores does not accurately distinguish more from less effective teachers because even relatively sophisticated approaches cannot adequately address the full range of statistical problems that arise in estimating a teacher's effectiveness. Efforts to address one statistical problem often introduce new ones. These challenges arise because of the influence of student socioeconomic advantage or disadvantage on learning, measurement error and instability, the nonrandom sorting of teachers across schools and of students to teachers in classrooms within schools, and the difficulty of disentangling the contributions of multiple teachers over time to students' learning. As a result, reliance on student test scores for evaluating teachers is likely to misidentify many teachers as either poor or successful.[37]

Concerns about the inaccuracy of ratings, along with incentives to narrow the curriculum, avoid high-need students, and replace cooperation with competition, inspired more than one-third of New York State's principals, plus 6,500 other educators and parents, to sign a letter protesting the adoption of the state's test-based evaluation system.[38]

The potential unintended consequences associated with high-stakes use of student test scores are illustrated by the response of

Susan Saunders, an expert teacher in Springfield, Massachusetts, to a proposed plan to evaluate and pay teachers based on their value-added test scores. Springfield is a high-minority, low-income district that had gone through huge budget cuts over many years. Fiscal woes had prevented salary increases for 3 years, and about half of the 2,600 teachers in the district had left over this time. Nearly 25% of the teaching force was uncertified and inexperienced.

Saunders, a Springfield native with more than 20 years of experience, had stayed and worked tirelessly to assist the revolving door of beginning teachers. A highly respected veteran, she gave the only remaining textbooks to the new teachers, and took on the highest-need special education students (comprising more than half of her class of 32 students) because she was able to work with them successfully. When asked how she would feel about working in this new system of test-based merit pay, Saunders said the introduction of the system would cause her to look for a job outside of teaching. In the meantime, she said, she would have to stop taking on the special education students and sharing materials with the other teachers in her building, because one teacher's success would come at the expense of another teacher's rating.

The evaluation system was not adopted, because a court-appointed arbitrator deemed the technical validity of the proposed system inadequate to carry the weight of personnel decision making. The investigation into the proposed system indicated that it could not produce accurate ratings. In addition to being accurate, however, it is critical that evaluation systems produce the right incentives for teaching. Good systems must be designed so that teachers are not discouraged from collaborating with one another or from teaching the students who have the greatest educational needs. Rather, they should explicitly seek to provide incentives that recognize and reward teachers who work together on behalf of needy students.

> **Good systems must be designed so that teachers are not discouraged from collaborating with one another or from teaching the students who have the greatest educational needs.**

From the perspective of incentives, test-based merit pay is especially problematic: Not only have two recent large-scale evaluations found that such schemes fail to improve student achievement,[39] it is possible that they can undermine activities that would support achievement. For example, when a study of Portugal's efforts to tie teacher pay to student test scores found that the system appeared to decrease student achievement, the researcher hypothesized that it may have reduced teacher collaboration to the detriment of student learning.[40] As *Washington Post* writer Jay Mathews has noted, leaders of effective schools are wary of individual test-based merit pay, because "their staffs thrive on teamwork. Everyone shares lesson plans, swaps ideas and reinforces discipline to help each child." They worry that big checks to just a few members of the team could ruin that collaboration and sense being a team.[41]

Although value-added measures of test-score gains may provide useful data for some teachers, to understand teachers' influences on student learning, more information about teachers' practices and context is needed. Student learning evidence needs to be multifaceted and accompanied by an analysis of the teacher's students and teaching context. (See box: Criteria for Using Measures of Student Learning in Teacher Evaluations.) It must be integrated with evidence about teachers' practice, and its use should be focused on improving teaching. In the next section, I discuss methods for achieving these goals.

CRITERIA FOR USING MEASURES OF STUDENT LEARNING IN TEACHER EVALUATIONS

1. **Assessment of teachers' contributions to student learning should rely on multiple measures of student learning, not a single test or value-added score.** Researchers have found that teaching effectiveness ratings are affected by which measures of learning are used. VAM estimates using different tests thus produce different results. In addition, no single test measures all the important aspects of teaching and learning, and most state tests measure a limited domain using spring-to-spring measures that add summer-learning-loss for low-income students to the other sources of error in looking at potential teacher effects. This will continue to be a problem when new tests produced by the two recently-established assessment consortia are available (the PARCC and Smarter Balanced Assessment Consortia).

As a consequence, the system of evaluation should include multiple measures of student learning, which can be collected at the classroom, school, or district level, and which evaluate a broad range of desired outcomes in different ways. Some of these might be tests. Others should be papers, projects, exhibitions, or portfolios of student work that demonstrate applied understanding. Some might be fall-to-spring measures (e.g., scored essays at the beginning and end of the year); others might show students' revisions of their products, illustrating growth during the teaching and learning process; still others might be periodic progress indicators using tools such as the Developmental Reading Assessment.

2. **Measures of learning should reflect the curriculum a teacher is expected to teach and the range of skills and competencies students are expected to develop.** Teachers should be evaluated on measures that evaluate the curriculum they teach—not a remote proxy. This might include external measures—such as Advanced Placement or International Baccalaureate tests for AP or IB teachers—or classroom, department, or school measures. in addition, teachers can be expected to focus on the kinds of learning that are included in evaluations. Thus, the collection of assessments should reflect the range of curriculum goals, including higher-order thinking and performance skills, such as writing, investigation, research, and problem solving. Measures should be continuously evaluated to determine the extent to which they address the range of knowledge and skills sought and their ability to capture student learning authentically and encourage the development of important skills.

3. **Valid measures should be used for all students,** including those with special needs or limited English proficiency, as well as students achieving below or above grade level. This means that assessments should measure the full continuum of achievement where possible, and may need to be differentiated to be appropriate for some students. For example, measures of English language proficiency growth might be included for teachers who are working with new English learners, and adapted assessments may be appropriate for some students with special education needs.

4. **Test measures intended to indicate growth must capture learning validly at the student's actual achievement level.** To evaluate how much a student has learned over a period of time, the assessment measures must reflect student performance at the level where a student actually achieves and measure changes accurately. Tests that measure only grade-level standards do not measure learning gains for students who are achieving below or above grade level. A test that has a low ceiling will not reveal gains made by students near the top of the distribution, and a test that has a high

(Continued)

floor will not measure what might be substantial gains made by students who are achieving below that level. Thus, the teachers who teach these students will be disadvantaged in value-added comparisons even if statistical adjustments are made. A measure of learning that can evaluate students along a continuous scale, such as the Developmental Reading Assessment (K–8) or the Qualitative Reading Inventory (K–12) will be more useful than a state test that measures standards in only a single grade level that fails to capture many students' growth and progress. Use of various measures should recognize the information offered by and limitations of each.

5. **The use of any student learning measure should take into account factors that affect student achievement gains, including characteristics of the students and of the context.** In addition to students' prior achievement, particular learning needs, and attendance, such factors should include aspects of the home context (e.g., poverty, homelessness) and classroom composition (e.g., percentage of new English learners, students who are advanced or who have been retained in grade), which greatly affects teachers' value-added scores. Other factors that may make a significant difference include class size, the quality and availability of curriculum materials, whether students also receive tutoring or related instruction from another teacher, and so on. This kind of information should be taken into account both in value-added analyses and in the overall compilation of information for an evaluation judgment.

6. **Value-added measures should be used only when there is a sufficient sample size and multiple years of data.** Studies find that many teachers have few students linked to them for whom data are available for both prior-year and current-year achievement. Other students who are mobile may have spent only a short time in a given teacher's classroom. Both of these are sources of considerable error. Year-to-year instability in teacher rankings is also very high. Many experts suggest that there should be at least 50 students (who have been with the teacher for a large majority of the year in each case) and at least 3 years of data to use in estimating a value-added score. Even with these considerations, it is important to recognize that multiple years of data may mask the year-to-year instability of scores, but do not eliminate the causes of such instability, which often include the composition of classes that teachers teach. Furthermore, more stable scores—whether relatively high or low—may simply reveal that teachers serve similar types of students from year to year, not that the estimate is a truer indication of teacher effectiveness.

7. **The evaluation system should consider evidence about student performance *and* teacher practice in an integrated fashion.** In order

to identify how a teacher's practices are connected to and influence student learning, the system must look at both together, along with information about the students who are being served. Teacher evaluation must triangulate information about students, teaching, and outcomes, just as the evaluation of doctors considers patient outcomes in light of patient characteristics and the doctor's expertise in enacting professional standards of practice. An integrated evaluation of practice and outcomes is also necessary to reduce ambiguity in attributing gains in student learning to a particular teacher's contribution. Any evaluation based on outcome measures faces considerable challenges in distinguishing between the results of instruction a classroom teacher provides and the instruction provided by prior teachers, other concurrent teachers, resource specialists, or tutors. In evaluating teacher performance, linking what students have learned to what a teacher actually did in the classroom is critically important.

8. **Various kinds of student learning data should be considered in the evaluation process commensurate with their limitations.** Given the large error range and instability associated with value-added estimates, and the fact that they represent many factors other than the individual teacher, it is clear that such estimates should be treated as error-prone. Because they will be extremely inaccurate for some subsets of teachers, they should not carry a pre-specified weight. Other data, whether classroom-based or external to the classroom, may also have specific limitations with respect to what is measured and what can be inferred from the evidence. For this reason, any source of data should always be considered in conjunction with other evidence of student learning and teacher practice.

9. **The use of student learning evidence should be a source of continual study for educators, researchers, and systems.** Independent researchers should continually examine teacher evaluation systems and results to identify questions and problems and to suggest improvements. There should be a regular, thorough analysis of all evaluation data, including test estimates if they are used, to examine whether different measures (based on different tests or other learning evidence, different measures of teacher performance, or different models for analyzing and combining data) provide different estimates. Given all the questions about what VAM estimates measure, studies should be done annually to examine the congruence between VAM measures and other measures of student learning and teacher performance, without a presumption that VAM estimates are more accurate than other, more stable measures.

PRODUCTIVE USES OF STUDENT LEARNING EVIDENCE

The shortcomings of current value-added analyses do not mean that districts cannot recognize and reward teachers for producing strong student learning, or create incentives for them to help other teachers and serve the neediest students. As we have already seen, it is possible to use other measures of student learning in evaluations of teaching, such as pre- and posttests of learning conducted at the classroom, school, or district level, or a range of learning evidence assembled by teachers themselves.

> **Shortcomings of value-added analysis do not mean that districts cannot recognize and reward teachers for producing strong student learning.**

Such evidence can be drawn from classroom assessments and documentation, or pre- and posttest measures of student learning in specific courses or curriculum areas (developed by individual teachers, departments, school faculty, or district faculty). Other possibilities include evidence of student accomplishments in relation to teaching activities, such as scored literary essays, student science investigations, history research papers, or art portfolios. Some districts use evidence from teachers' careful documentation of the learning of a set of diverse students over time, like that included in National Board Certification portfolios. (See the Appendix for an example.)

Analysis of standardized test results could be included, where valid and appropriate for the curriculum and the students being taught. Different assessments may be needed for different students— for example, English-language proficiency tests for new English learners and measures related to individual education plans (IEPs) or alternative assessments for some special education students. For some classes, Advanced Placement (AP) tests or International Baccalaureate (IB) tests linked to the curriculum being taught could be appropriate. Such evidence could come from instruments developed at the school, district, state, national, or even international levels. In Carolyn Abbott's case, for example, the Regents Integrated Algebra tests that her students studied for would be a logical part of the body of evidence about her students' learning. Where they are used, tests should always constitute only one part of a broader array of data, including student work.

The evidence can be assembled by the teacher in a teaching portfolio, demonstrating and explaining the progress of students on a wide range of learning outcomes in ways that take students' starting points and characteristics into account. In some schools, teachers use their own fall and spring classroom assessments as a way of gauging student progress, including measures tailored to the learning goals of specific students (for example, special education students or English language learners). Some schools and districts have common assessments that are used in particular grades and courses. As part of a portfolio of evidence, such measures can document teaching effectiveness in achieving specific curriculum goals.

Measures of student learning in specific subject areas may include scored writing samples or research projects (including first to last drafts), miscue analyses and other documentation of students' reading over time, or even musical performances. These measures typically provide better indications of student learning in a specific course or subject area because they are curriculum-specific. They are also more likely to capture the effects of a particular teacher's instruction and be available for most or all students. A teacher might even document the Westinghouse science competition awards she helped students win, or specific breakthroughs achieved by her students, with evidence of her role in supporting these accomplishments.

Goal-Setting and Evaluating Student Learning

In a growing number of states and districts, evaluation systems ask teachers to set goals for their students on one or more dimensions of their learning, based on initial information about their achievement, and then to evaluate progress toward these goals, using a variety of measures.

Some innovative teacher evaluation programs have long included strategies like this using various types of evidence of student learning. In Rochester's career ladder, for example, evidence of student learning, determined by the teacher, is assembled in the teacher's portfolio. In Denver's *Procomp* system,[42] teachers set two goals annually in collaboration with the principal, and document student progress toward these goals using district-, school-, or teacher-created assessments to show growth. In Arizona, districts have created several different strategies for setting goals and aggregating data about student learning gains. (See examples in Chapter 4.)

In award-winning Long Beach, California, a predominantly minority district widely recognized for its strong achievement and steady reduction of achievement gaps, teachers set goals for student progress as individuals, as teams within departments or grade levels, and at the school level. These data supplement the information about their practice, based on standards-based observations of their performance in relation to the California Standards for the Teaching Profession. Progress toward teachers' individual and group goals is taken into account in both self-evaluations and supervisory evaluations. The evaluatee proposes how achievement of his or her objectives can be assessed, using evidence such as:

> **In award-winning Long Beach, California, teachers set goals as individuals, as teams, and at the school level.**

- Teacher observation and judgment
- Anecdotal and cumulative records
- Success and progress on a continuum of learning or a course of study
- Teacher-, department-, or school-made tests for pretesting and posttesting
- Curriculum-related tests
- Use of audiovisual documentation if desired and available
- Student self-evaluations
- Evaluative discussion with students and parents
- Records of students' past learning performances
- Files of students' work collected to show growth
- Action research[43]

The district creates explicit and ongoing opportunities for schools, departments, and grade-level teams to review student work and test score data of various kinds, to evaluate progress within and across classrooms, to discuss curriculum and teaching strategies, to problem solve around the needs of individuals and groups of students, and to plan for improvements.

Data analysis practices in Long Beach reflect what National Board Certified teacher Renee Moore suggests when she argues:

> I would suggest that one important component of new student assessments is that the results be given not just to the individual teachers of those students, but that teachers be involved in the interpretation and discussion of test data together, in various configurations. . . . This type of data interpretation would be, in fact, a form of de facto peer evaluation.[44]

One outcome of these problem-solving processes in Long Beach is that the most expert teachers are encouraged to take on the highest-need students. Because gifted veterans can often move such students forward furthest, the students gain much more than they otherwise would. Meanwhile, other teachers who have easier classes can experience greater success, and everyone wins. Superintendent Chris Steinhauser believes that the use of state test-score gains in individual teacher evaluations would undermine the district's successful practices by penalizing teachers for taking on the toughest assignments and by undermining teacher collaboration. Instead, in Long Beach, the teacher evaluation system supports a culture of collective improvement.

Recent State Initiatives. Some states and districts have adopted systems of *Student Learning Objectives (SLOs)* as a means for structuring a goal-setting process in which teachers assemble learning evidence to evaluate how students are making progress. Conceptually, the notion of SLOs is intended to draw evidence that derives organically from the curriculum and the work of the classroom. A recent description from the American Institute of Research includes:

- Performance-based assessments, such as presentations, projects, and rubric-scored tasks;
- Portfolios of student work, with samples throughout the year that illustrate knowledge and skills before and after a learning experience;

- State or national tests;
- Educator, school-created, or district-created tests.[45]

Having chosen goals from the curriculum, linked to the standards, teachers set specific targets on assessment measures—for entire classrooms and/or specific subsets of students, for an entire course or a specific set of skills or content within the course—taking into account students' starting points. The goals and evidence of student learning are examined, along with evidence of teachers' practices, in the evaluation process. This process also can be designed to enhance collegial problem-solving. In one vision:

> SLOs can be used to promote collaboration and reflection on practice among educators. Educators are not expected to work in isolation. By setting districtwide, subject-level, grade-level, or team-based SLOs, educators can establish common learning targets for their students and work together to meet the needs of all students. Furthermore, the SLO development cycle encourages educators to seek guidance and assistance from specialists who support student learning, including special education teachers; English language learner specialists; speech-language therapists; counselors; and curriculum, assessment, and data specialists.[46]

This potentially valuable approach has, however, evolved in different ways across states and districts. In some cases, SLOs have been conceptualized narrowly, focusing primarily on more standardized tests used to rank individual teachers against each other. However, other states have insisted on maintaining a broader conception of learning and a closer link to classroom practices. In Rhode Island, for instance, the Department of Education has insisted that SLOs should not require teachers to create or use new assessments, but to select high-quality assessments embedded in the curriculum that measure the most important learning that occurs within the grade or subject.[47] Examplars of SLOs offered on the Department website include those that feature portfolios and performance tasks, as well as essays and other forms of student work.[48]

Both Oregon and Washington State are working to develop statewide systems that include this kind of goal-setting and assessment using multiple measures of student learning. In Oregon, for example, teachers, along with their supervisors, establish at least two student learning goals and identify strategies and measures that will be used to determine goal attainment. They also specify what pieces of evidence (at least two) will document progress on each goal, including classroom-based and external measures, based on what is most appropriate for the curriculum and students they teach. At the end of the year, an analysis and reflection on results seeks to identify what strategies, supports, and resources worked and what other strategies might be pursued in the future.

Massachusetts' new teacher evaluation system, collaboratively developed by the State Department of Education and the Massachusetts Teachers Association, incorporates evidence of student learning selected through a goal-setting process for teachers, combined with evidence of teacher practice in the classroom and with families, and evidence of professional contributions. The measures used to evaluate the standards include observations and artifacts of teaching, documentation of activities and outcomes, multiple sources of evidence about student learning, and student feedback. The system is designed to ensure that the evidence is considered in a fully integrated way, with no weights or fixed percentages for any single source of data, and with the goal of ensuring that teacher learning is supported. (See box: Massachusetts' Multiple Measures System of Evaluation.)

MASSACHUSETTS' MULTIPLE MEASURES SYSTEM OF EVALUATION

Massachusetts has adopted a multiple measures system of evaluation for both teachers and administrators that considers practice, professional contributions, and student outcomes in an integrated process. The standards for teachers focus on the following:

1. **Curriculum, Planning, and Assessment**: Promotes the learning and growth of all students by providing high-quality and coherent instruction, designing and administering authentic and meaningful student assessments, analyzing student performance and growth data, using this data to improve instruction, providing students with constructive feedback on an ongoing basis, and continuously refining learning objectives.

2. **Teaching All Students**: Promotes the learning and growth of all students through instructional practices that establish high expectations,

(Continued)

create a safe and effective classroom environment, and demonstrate cultural proficiency.

3. **Family and Community Engagement**: Promotes the learning and growth of all students through effective partnerships with families, caregivers, community members, and organizations.

4. **Professional Culture**: Promotes the learning and growth of all students through ethical, culturally proficient, skilled, and collaborative practice.

The collection of evidence used in the evaluation includes:

1. Multiple measures of student learning, including measures of student progress on classroom assessments aligned with the state standards; measures of student progress on learning goals set between the educator and evaluator for the school year; and district or state measures where appropriate and available

2. Judgments about practice based on observations and artifacts of teaching

3. Evidence of professional responsibilities and growth, such as self-assessments, peer collaboration, professional development linked to goals and or educator plans, and contributions to the school community and professional culture

4. Evidence of active outreach to and ongoing engagement with families

5. Student feedback with respect to teachers, and staff feedback with respect to administrators

There are no fixed percentages for any single source of data. Data are combined and ratings from unsatisfactory to exemplary are determined using multiple categories of evidence with either the state-developed rubric or one approved by the state.

Source: *http://www.doe.mass.edu/lawsregs/603cmr35.html?section=07.*

As the Massachusetts system and others I have described indicate, it is possible to create evaluation systems that include a wide range of learning outcomes and teaching activities that are valued and encouraged by the process of evaluation. One critically important feature of productive strategies is that they require teachers to collect, examine, interpret, and use evidence about student learning to reflect on and plan instruction, and to inform improvements. Equally important are the incentives and opportunities for ongoing professional learning that give teachers the knowledge and skills that allow them to respond to evidence of student learning in ever-more-effective ways. I turn to this issue in the next chapter.

6 Support Meaningful Professional Learning

[There] is increasing consensus that the most effective forms of professional development are those that are directly related to teachers' instructional practice, intensive and sustained, integrated with school-reform efforts, and that actively engage teachers in collaborative professional communities.

—Ruth Chung Wei and Colleagues[1]

I'd like to see the teacher evaluation process become meaningful in terms of teacher growth. . . . [For example], I worked with a group of teachers on an action research project. We wanted to know how intermediate students learn more from one another through classroom conversations. One teacher who had never let students do much talking began to change his practice over time so that after several months students were regularly engaging in questioning and challenging one another. He began to see much deeper levels of understanding from all of the students. He admitted that if he had not had the examples and support of colleagues, he would still be stuck in a "sage on the stage" model of teaching.

—Kathie Marshall, Teacher Leaders Network Fellow and
Disney Creative Classroom Award Winner[2]

Finally, it is important to link both formal professional development and job-embedded learning opportunities to the evaluation system. Evaluation alone will not improve practice. Productive feedback must be accompanied by opportunities to learn. Evaluations should trigger continuous goal-setting for areas teachers want to work on, specific professional development supports and coaching, and opportunities to share expertise, as part of recognizing teachers' strengths and needs. As earlier chapters illustrate, evaluation can

> **Productive feedback must be accompanied by opportunities to learn.**

be used to stimulate meaningful professional learning as teachers set goals and pursue them with the assistance of administrators and colleagues. In addition, it can be used to flag areas for further support that are made available through a cycle of ongoing professional development.

It is also important that we revise our notion of what kinds of opportunities support professional growth. As a recent report from the National Staff Development Council noted, professional learning can be a result of:

> both formal professional development and other opportunities for professional learning—such as common planning time, shared opportunities to examine student work, or tools for self-reflection—that may occur outside the bounds of formal professional development events. . . . Professional learning [is] a product of both externally-provided and job-embedded activities that increase teachers' knowledge and change their instructional practice in ways that support student learning. Thus, formal professional development represents a subset of the range of experiences that may result in professional learning.[3]

> **Whereas less than 14 hours per year on a given topic had no effect on student learning, high-quality professional development programs averaging about 50 hours over a 6- to 12-month period increased student achievement by 21 percentile points.**

It is critical that professional learning opportunities be of high quality. Rather than the drive-by, spray-and-pray, flavor-of-the-month after school workshops that predominate in the United States, teachers should have access to the kind of sustained, focused learning that has been shown to improve practice. For example, a review of experimental studies found that whereas professional development offerings of less than 14 hours per year on a given topic had no effect on student learning, high-quality professional development programs averaging about 50 hours over a 6- to 12-month period increased student achievement by 21 percentile points on average.[4] These high-quality opportunities are typically:

- focused on the learning and teaching of specific curriculum content,
- organized around real problems of practice,
- connected to teachers' work with children,
- linked to analysis of teaching and student learning,
- intensive, sustained, and continuous over time,
- supported by coaching, modeling, observation, and feedback,
- connected to teachers' collaborative work in professional learning communities, and
- integrated into school and classroom planning around curriculum, instruction, and assessment.

Such opportunities may include intensive institutes focused on particular strategies or on the teaching of specific curriculum, interspersed with opportunities for teachers to try things in the classroom, receive coaching, reflect together on their experiences, revise and revamp their approaches, and develop increasingly polished skills in an iterative cycle of practice, reflection, and fine-tuning. They may include opportunities to analyze observations or videos of teaching and/or samples of student work, study groups, action research projects, peer observations, and collaborative planning and evaluation in grade-level or departmental teams.[5]

The large potential gains from such work should certainly make redesign of a district's professional development worthwhile. Because effective professional learning is tied to real classroom practice, it also has the advantage of supporting teachers in what they are doing rather than taking time for essentially ineffective isolated trainings.

However, this kind of professional development is relatively rare in the United States. National data show that although most teachers participate in some kind of professional development each year, very few have the chance to study any aspect of teaching for more than a day or two. And fewer than half are involved in any kind of mentoring, coaching, or collaborative research.[6] Even though mentoring programs for beginning teachers are becoming more common, only about half of novices receive regular mentoring from a teacher in their teaching field or have common planning time with other teachers.[7]

Short workshops of the sort generally found to trigger little change in practice are the most common learning opportunity for U.S. teachers. In 2008, for example, whereas more than 80% of teachers engaged in professional development regarding subject-matter content, fewer than 25% experienced more than 32 hours of professional learning in this area during the year. Sixty percent of teachers received some professional development in reading instruction, but fewer than 20% worked on these issues for two days or more. Fewer than half of U.S. teachers received even 8 hours of professional development on strategies for teaching students with disabilities or English language learners, despite the strong desire teachers voice for more learning opportunities in these areas.[8]

PROFESSIONAL LEARNING THAT PAYS OFF

A great deal more is known today than was once the case about the features of professional learning that improve teaching practice and student learning. The four features described here are particularly important.[9]

1. Professional development should be intensive, ongoing, and connected to practice. As noted, most professional development for teachers still comes in the form of occasional workshops, typically lasting a day or two at most, each one focusing on discrete topics (such as classroom management, reading instruction, use of technology, or how to use a particular textbook series), with their connection to classroom practice left to teachers' imaginations. However, such episodic workshops disconnected from practice do not allow teachers the time needed for rigorous and cumulative study of the given subject matter, for seeing exemplars or receiving coaching, or for trying out ideas in the classroom and reflecting on the results.

> **A great deal more is known today than was once the case about the features of professional learning that improve teaching practice and student learning.**

Research that finds changes in teacher practice supports this commonsense conclusion: Intensive and sustained professional development activities, especially when they include applications of knowledge to teachers' planning and instruction, have a greater chance of influencing teaching practices and, in turn, leading to gains in student learning.[10] Indeed, greater duration of a professional development activity appears to be associated with a stronger impact on teachers and student learning, in part perhaps because such sustained efforts typically include applications to practice, often supported by study groups and/or coaching.

In addition to the experimental studies noted earlier, two separate evaluations of a year-long program designed to promote inquiry-based science instruction found that teachers who received 80 or more hours of professional development were significantly more likely to put the desired teaching strategies into practice than were teachers who had received many fewer hours. Further, the more exposure teachers had to those professional development activities, the greater the achievement gains posted by their students during the following year.[11]

These findings resonate with teachers' beliefs about the value of intensive and ongoing professional development programs. According to results from national surveys, teachers view inservice activities as most effective when they are sustained over time,[12] and they rate professional development as most useful to them when it is longer in duration.[13]

2. Professional development should focus on the teaching and learning of specific academic content. Research suggests that professional development activities are most effective when they address the concrete, everyday challenges involved in teaching and learning specific academic subject matter, rather than focusing on abstract educational principles or teaching methods taken out of context. For example, researchers have found that teachers are more likely to try classroom practices that have been modeled for them in professional development settings.[14] Likewise, teachers themselves judge professional development to be most valuable when it provides opportunities to do "hands-on" work that builds their knowledge of academic content and how to teach it to their students, and when it takes into account the local context (including specific school resources, curriculum guidelines, accountability systems, and so on).[15]

Equally important, professional development that leads teachers to define precisely which concepts and skills they want students to learn, and to identify the content that is most likely to give students trouble, has been found to improve teacher practice and student outcomes.[16] To this end, it is often useful for teachers to be put in the position of studying the very material that they intend to teach to their own students. For example, one well-known study focused on elementary science teachers who participated in a 100-hour summer institute, during which they actively engaged in a standard "learning cycle," which involved exploring a phenomenon, coming up with a theory that explains what has occurred, and applying it to new contexts. After going through this process, teachers went on to develop their own units and teach them to one another before returning to their classrooms. Later, the researchers tested randomly selected students in those classrooms and found they scored 44% higher on an assessment of scientific reasoning than did a control group of students taught by teachers who had not participated in the summer institute.[17]

It can also be useful for groups of teachers to analyze and discuss student performance data and samples of students' work (science projects, essays, math problems, and so on), in order to identify students' most common errors and misunderstandings, reach common understanding of what it means for students to master a given concept or skill, and find out which instructional strategies are or are not working, and for whom.[18] Notably, one study of three high-achieving schools found that high levels of student performance seemed to be associated in part with teachers' regular practice of consulting multiple sources of data on student performance and using those data to inform discussions about ways to improve instruction.[19]

> It can be useful for groups of teachers to analyze and discuss student performance data and samples of students' work to identify common errors and misunderstandings, reach common understanding of what it means for students to master a given concept or skill, and find out which instructional strategies are or are not working, and for whom.

3. Professional development should be connected to other school initiatives. Research suggests that professional development tends to be more effective when it is an integral part of a larger school reform effort, rather than when activities are isolated, having little to do with other initiatives or changes under way at the school.[20] If teachers sense a disconnect between what they are urged to do in a workshop and what they are required to do under local curriculum guidelines, texts, assessment practices, and so on—that is, if they cannot easily implement the strategies they learn, and the new practices are not supported or reinforced—then the professional development tends to have little impact.

One prominent model of carefully integrated professional development was the National Science Foundation's *Discovery* program implemented in Ohio, which offered sustained support for teachers as part of a larger statewide effort to improve student achievement in science. Following intensive 6-week institutes focusing on science content and instruction, connected to the state standards, teachers were given release time to attend a series of six seminars, focusing on curriculum and assessment. In addition, they were provided on-demand support and site visits from regional staff developers, and contact with peers through newsletters and annual conferences. According to an independent evaluation, this combination of support led to a significant increase in and continued use of inquiry-based instructional practices in line with the science initiative promoted across the state.[21]

4. Professional development should build strong working relationships among teachers. Given the design of factory-model schools, American teachers have rarely had the opportunity to join each other in planning lessons, providing instruction, assessing students, designing curriculum, or helping to make administrative or managerial decisions. However, research shows that when schools are strategic and persistent in creating productive working relationships within academic departments, across them, or among teachers schoolwide, the benefits can include greater consistency in instruction, more willingness to share practices and try new ways of teaching, and more success in solving problems of practice.[22]

> **Perhaps the simplest way to break down professional isolation is for teachers to observe each other's teaching and to provide constructive feedback.**

Perhaps the simplest way to break down professional isolation is for teachers to observe each other's teaching and to provide constructive feedback. In an evaluation of schools

> **Large-scale studies have identified specific ways in which professional community-building can deepen teachers' knowledge, build their skills, and improve instruction.**

implementing Critical Friends Groups—a peer-observation system developed by the National Reform Faculty, including a set of protocols that teachers use to guide their observations and responses— researchers found that teachers' instruction became more student-centered, with a focus on ensuring that students gained mastery of the subject as opposed to merely covering the material. Teachers in these schools also reported having more opportunities to learn and a greater desire to continuously develop more effective practices than teachers who did not participate.[23]

Several large-scale studies have identified specific ways in which professional community-building can deepen teachers' knowledge, build their skills, and improve instruction.[24] For example, a comprehensive 5-year study of 1,500 schools undergoing major reforms found that in schools where teachers formed active professional learning communities, achievement increased significantly in math, science, history, and reading, while student absenteeism and dropout rates were reduced. Further, particular aspects of teachers' professional community—a shared sense of intellectual purpose and a sense of collective responsibility for student learning—were associated with a narrowing of achievement gaps in math and science among low- and middle-income students.[25]

> **Strong professional learning communities require leadership that establishes a vision, creates opportunities and expectations, and finds the resources needed.**

Strong professional learning communities require leadership that establishes a vision, creates opportunities and expectations for joint work, and finds the resources needed to support the work, including expertise and time to meet.[26]

Collaborative teacher teams can productively engage in collective inquiry into their practice by:

- examining data on student progress,
- analyzing student work,

- determining effective strategies to facilitate learning,
- designing and critiquing curriculum units and lessons,
- observing and coaching one another, and
- developing and scoring common classroom-based assessments to measure progress.[27]

Over time, this work can be more deeply supported if professional learning opportunities are conceptualized as part of a career continuum that encourages teachers to gain and share expertise. Productive career ladders (or lattices) can also create avenues for such sharing to occur, as teachers take on roles as mentor and master teachers, as curriculum and assessment specialists, and as leaders of school-improvement activities.

BUILDING COLLECTIVE EXPERTISE

The challenge of getting to scale with good educational practice[28] is in developing widespread educational leadership and expert teaching on the one hand, and encouraging the design of effective organizations on a system-wide scale on the other. The work of improving practice must therefore be conceptualized as collective rather than individual.

> **The work of improving practice must be conceptualized as collective rather than individual.**

Although opportunities to study and learn specific strategies that are central to individual practice are important, and may be pursued through specific coursework or participation in subject-matter networks or conferences, it is also important to create collective capacity and curriculum coherence among the staff members in a school.

A particularly focused approach is that used by the Teacher Advancement Program (TAP). Although TAP was originally touted largely as an innovative compensation system, because it ties a component of salary increases to evaluations, what teachers have found most useful about the program is its system of continuous feedback tied to collaboration time and professional development.[29] In fact, a survey of teacher attitudes in TAP schools found that 70% were very enthusiastic about the dimensions of the program that support collegiality; 60% found the job-embedded approach to professional development very helpful; and 57% were very supportive of the teacher evaluation system, as it was being implemented, with 76% saying they frequently used the feedback they received to improve their practice. However, only 18% were enthusiastic about the performance pay component, suggesting that this is not the most important incentive for teacher improvement.[30]

TAP's evaluation instrument was developed based on the standards of the National Board and INTASC and the assessment rubrics developed in Connecticut and Rochester, New York, among others.[31] In the TAP system of "instructionally focused accountability," each teacher is evaluated four to six times a year by master/mentor teachers who have climbed the TAP career ladder based on evidence of their teaching effectiveness as well as by principals who are trained and certified evaluators. The training is a rigorous 4-day process, and trainers must be certified based on their ability to evaluate teaching accurately and reliably. In readiness for using the system, teachers also study the rubric and its implications for teaching and learning, look at and evaluate videotaped teaching episodes using the rubric, and engage in practice evaluations. After each observation, the evaluator and teacher meet to discuss the findings and to make a plan for ongoing growth.

TAP integrates ongoing professional development, mentoring, and classroom support to help teachers meet these standards:

> Sessions are led by master and mentor teachers who explain the instructional practices measured by the TAP Teaching Standards. They model such practices in professional development meetings (known as "clusters") and in the classroom. This is where the core collaboration happens. Teachers analyze student data and learn new instructional strategies to improve student learning. Master teachers select the strategies based on detailed analyses of student achievement data. . . . After master teachers introduce a new strategy, teachers use it in their own classrooms, then they have cluster meetings appointed with formative assessment data from before and after the strategies were adopted. They discuss how well the strategy worked, then refine it if necessary.[32]

Master and mentor teachers also coach teachers individually, engage in modeling and demonstration lessons, and meet with teachers outside of class. Teachers in TAP schools report that these opportunities, along with the intensive professional development offered, are substantially responsible for improvements in their practice and the gains in student achievement that have occurred in many TAP schools.[33] To support this work, TAP reorganizes its schools to provide regular time for collaborative planning and learning.

Creating Time for Collaborative Planning and Learning

Indeed, the best systems typically create time for teachers to work and learn together during the school day, as is common in high-achieving nations in Europe and Asia, where teachers typically have 15 to 25 hours a week to plan and work together.[34] According to the Organization for Economic Cooperation and Development (OECD), more than 85% of schools in Belgium, Denmark, Finland, Hungary, Ireland, Norway, Sweden, and Switzerland provide time for professional development in teachers' work day or week.[35] Over time, this collective investment reaps greater gains for student learning than the efforts of any one teacher alone.

> **The best systems typically create time for teachers to work and learn together during the school day, as is common in high-achieving nations in Europe and Asia.**

U.S. teachers have more net teaching time—more than 1000 hours per year—than teachers in the other OECD countries, far greater than the OECD average of 800 hours per year for primary schools and 660 hours per year for upper secondary schools.[36] Thus, whereas teachers in high-achieving nations spend about half of their time preparing and learning to teach well, most U.S. teachers have little or no time to work with colleagues during the school day. They typically receive only about

> **Whereas teachers in high-achieving nations spend about half of their time preparing and learning to teach well, most U.S. teachers have little or no time to work with colleagues.**

3 to 5 hours weekly in which to plan by themselves, and they get a few "hit-and-run" workshops after school, with little opportunity to share knowledge or improve their practice. According to a 2009 Met Life survey, American teachers average only 2.7 hours per week for collaboration. And in 2008, only 16% of teachers reported that they experienced a great deal of cooperative effort among the staff in their schools, down from 34% in 2000.[37]

The lack of time for collaborative planning gives U.S. teachers less opportunity to develop sophisticated practice. Some restructured schools in the United States have tackled this problem by redesigning the use of time and resources to support student and teacher learning with longer periods, shared planning time, and extensive ongoing professional development. The major strategies for reorganizing time have included the following:

> **Lack of time for collaborative planning gives U.S. teachers less opportunity to develop sophisticated practice.**

- Staffing patterns that allocate more positions to classroom teaching, rather than to other kinds of supplementary staffing roles;
- More streamlined secondary school schedules that engage students with fewer teachers for longer blocks of time each day; and
- Organizational approaches that allow teachers to work in teams that serve a common group of students.[38]

Redesigned high schools have secured 7 to 10 hours of shared time per week by hiring more teachers and fewer nonteaching personnel; offering a more streamlined curriculum with fewer low-enrollment courses; organizing time in longer blocks, thus requiring reduced teaching loads; and using time when students are in clubs or internships for teacher collaboration.

Elementary schools have created a range of different models as well. At one school, teachers decided to teach four full days of academic classes each week and spend the fifth full day planning together with their teams and pursuing professional development, while their students rotated to resource classes in music, art, computer lab, physical education, library, and science lab. Other schools have found shared planning time by reducing specialization and pull-outs, integrating special education teachers into teams, and eliminating separate Title I classes to reduce the size of groups for all students. Other schools "bank" time by adding time onto each day so as to free up an afternoon for collaboration time; some organize recreation or afterschool activities for students so that teachers can plan together.[39]

It is possible to create the context for teachers to become more effective, but it may require thinking differently about some of the traditional "regularities of schooling."[40]

Creating a Framework for Continuous Learning

Schools and districts must develop conditions that provide teachers and principals with sufficient organizational and instructional support to carry out a system of teacher evaluation that enables continuous learning. For example, teachers and principals need the time and guidance to develop a shared understanding of effective teaching, to examine artifacts of practice for evidence of learning, to explore one another's assumptions about how learning occurs and what counts as evidence of learning, to promote reflection, and to learn how to provide effective feedback. Without these sorts of school-based conditions, the ability for a teacher evaluation program to stimulate ongoing professional learning is severely handicapped.

> **Teachers and principals need time and guidance to develop a shared understanding of effective teaching, to examine artifacts of practice for evidence of learning, to explore how learning occurs and what counts as evidence of learning, to promote reflection, and to learn how to provide effective feedback.**

Systems for sharing expertise are a key aspect of an effective system. The literacy and mathematics initiatives in Arkansas illustrate what can happen when a state becomes focused on supporting professional development. In 2005, the state increased its required hours of annual professional development from 30 to 60. These hours can include joint curriculum planning and work by teams to analyze student data. Several notable statewide professional development initiatives provide the kind of extended, collegial learning opportunities identified by research as needed for changing practice and outcomes.

Among these are a statewide cadre of expert literacy and mathematics specialists who provide targeted training to all schools and districts to implement standards-based instruction in reading, writing, and math. In mathematics, for example, specialists provide support and training for more than 200 teacher leaders and coaches across the state, who in turn support teachers in local schools. The state also offers a 5-day summer training course in "Math Solutions," which enrolls several hundred teachers each time it is offered. In between the courses, the state mathematics specialists provide follow-up, including additional classes, coaching, and collective problem solving, to help teachers put their learning to use in their daily instructional practice, honing their questioning skills and their ability to offer hands-on experiences. A Math Solutions specialist commented, "I don't know of any other state that has this system in place. . . . They are charting a new course for building capacity throughout the state." During the period between 2000 and 2005, 8th graders in Arkansas made among the largest gains in mathematics on the National Assessment of Education Progress, with especially large gains for African American students.[41] These gains have continued, and by 2011, the percentage of 4th graders achieving at the "basic" or above level on NAEP had increased to 81% from only 55% a decade earlier.[42]

To transform systems, incentives must be structured to promote collaboration and knowledge sharing, rather than competition, across organizations. Knowledge sharing is needed to develop not only learning organizations but a learning-oriented system of education.

> **Incentives must be structured to promote collaboration and knowledge sharing, rather than competition, across organizations.**

This has been the primary strategy for improvement in high-achieving Singapore, for example, where ongoing evaluation and inquiry into practice are stimulated within and across classrooms, across schools partnered within regions, and within the system as a whole.[43] (See box: Teacher Evaluation and Development in Singapore.)

TEACHER EVALUATION AND DEVELOPMENT IN SINGAPORE

Oon-Seng Tan, the dean of teacher education at the National Institute of Education (NIE) in Singapore, notes that the current U.S. focus on teacher evaluation "may unwittingly obscure the need for a holistic teacher development and evaluation process."[44] In Singapore, where teaching is a respected career with low turnover, and student outcomes are among the best in the world, "teacher evaluation and development [are] formative, not critical and summative."[45] Teacher learning is supported both by structured collegial inquiry opportunities and by career ladders that develop master teachers, curriculum and assessment specialists, and school leaders, who in turn support the development of other teachers along the career continuum.

Teachers are assessed each year by their principal and department head based on their contributions to the holistic development of students, including the quality of students' learning (based on classroom evidence), pastoral care and well-being of students, co-curricular activities, and collaboration with parents. Annual evaluations are used to identify ongoing steps for teachers' development, including eventual development into a master teacher, curriculum specialist, or school leader on one of Singapore's three career tracks.

The government pays for 100 hours of professional development each year for all teachers, in addition to the 20 hours a week teachers have to work and learn together. To support school-based learning, senior and master teachers are appointed to lead the coaching and development of the teachers in each school. NIE has worked with the Ministry of Education to train teachers to undertake action research projects in the classroom so they can examine teaching and learning problems and find solutions that can be disseminated to others.

Among Singapore's many investments in teacher professional learning is the Teacher's Network, established in 1998 by the Ministry as part of the "Thinking Schools, Learning Nation" initiative and now part of a new Academy that supports teacher development. The Teacher's Network serves as a catalyst for teacher-initiated development through sharing, collaboration, and reflection. The Network includes learning circles, teacher-led workshops, and conferences, as well as a website and publications series for sharing knowledge.[46]

In a Teacher's Network learning circle, 4 to 10 teachers and a facilitator collaboratively identify and solve common problems chosen by the participating teachers using discussions and action research. The learning circles generally meet for eight 2-hour sessions over a period of 4 to 12 months.

(Continued)

Supported by the national university, Teacher's Network professional development officers run an initial whole-school training program on the key processes of reflection, dialogue, and action research and a more extended program to train teachers as learning circle facilitators and mentor facilitators in the field.

A major part of the facilitator's role is to encourage the teachers to act as co-learners and critical friends so they feel safe to take the risks of sharing their assumptions and personal theories, experimenting with new ideas and practices, and sharing their successes and problems. Discussing problems and possible solutions in learning circles fosters a sense of collegiality among teachers and encourages teachers to be reflective practitioners. Learning circles allow teachers to feel that they are producing knowledge, not just disseminating received knowledge.

Where a collegial approach is used to support teachers, novices have help to advance to expert levels, students are exposed to sophisticated practices built by teachers working together, and administrators spend time building the success of an existing team rather than continually hiring new beginners.

Also key to developing such a system is the creation of networks that allow teachers, leaders, schools, and districts to learn from one another. Andy Hargreaves describes an initiative in England in which 300 schools that were declining in performance were networked with one another, provided with technical assistance and support from mentor schools, and given a small discretionary budget to support their efforts. Schools were also given a practitioner-generated list of strategies that had produced improvements in other schools. More than two-thirds of these "exceptionally energized" schools experienced gains over the next 2 years at rates double the national average, "without," the researchers noted, "the characteristic mandates and prescriptions that had characterized English reforms before this point."[47] An initiative in Ontario, Canada, used similar school-to-school networking strategies and leveraged them further by identifying positive exemplars that schools could visit to see successful reforms in action. As these examples indicate, when schools learn to create better conditions for teaching and learning, individual and collective teaching practice can improve.

7 Create Structures to Enable Fair and Effective Evaluation

In our country, I think we don't make evaluation a priority and we don't view it as a [means for] growth. It's either perfunctory or it's punitive, and that's the problem. If it's perfunctory then it's meaningless, and if it's punitive, then [teachers] react against it. And to get that sweet spot where people realize it's about getting everybody to improve and collaborate . . . that takes a lot of work.

—*Greg Jouriles, Teacher and Association Leader, San Mateo, California*

One serious shortcoming of teacher evaluation reforms is that they have often focused on designing instruments for observing teachers, without developing the structural elements of a sound evaluation system. These elements should include, at minimum:

- trained, skilled evaluators
- supports for teachers needing assistance
- governance structures that enable sound personnel decisions
- resources to sustain the system

In addition, systems should be designed to be manageable and feasible, not so complex that they overwhelm the participants with requirements and paperwork. I discuss these system features next.

EVALUATOR EXPERTISE

Strong evaluation systems need principals and other evaluators with deep knowledge of teaching and learning, as well as an understanding of how to evaluate teaching, how to give useful feedback, and how to plan professional development that supports teacher learning. The lack of such knowledge and training has

> **The lack of knowledge and training has been a major problem for the validity, fairness, and utility of many teacher evaluation systems.**

been a major problem for the validity, fairness, and utility of many teacher evaluation systems. The answers to these needs are severalfold:

- **Stronger principal preparation** coupled with the use of performance-based licensure for principals. Connecticut's approach is a good example: Principal preparation is focused on instructional leadership, teacher supervision, and professional development. Performance-based licensing assessments require principals to demonstrate that they can evaluate videotapes of teaching accurately and then plan appropriate feedback and professional supports.
- **Specific, intensive training in evaluation and supervision.** Training for evaluators is conducted in states such as Connecticut and in programs like the Teacher Advancement Program, which offers several days of training for principals in the use of the standards-based evaluation tools and strategies for providing useful feedback and follow-up.
- **Involvement of lead teachers with content expertise** in some aspects of supervision and evaluation. For example, some districts involve department chairpersons or other lead teachers matched to teachers' content areas.

Stronger Principal Preparation

In a recent study, my colleagues and I documented major differences between principal preparation programs that were identified as producing highly effective graduates and those that most principals have experienced.[1] Among the key differences were the exemplary programs' strong emphases on developing the knowledge and hands-on skills for instructional leadership, including the capacity to understand and analyze instruction, provide useful feedback, and design professional learning. If principal preparation programs were routinely designed to accomplish this, teachers would have many more opportunities for effective learning.

The state of Connecticut took a particularly productive approach to upgrading principals' instructional knowledge and skills. When it undertook statewide teacher education reforms that raised salaries and standards for teaching in the late 1980s, Connecticut also raised standards for principals—and tied principals' training to their capacity to support and evaluate teachers. Principals were trained to evaluate teachers in the beginning teacher performance assessment system (the BEST assessment described in Chapter 2), as well as a then-new local evaluation system for veteran teachers. They received credit toward re-licensure for their participation in assessment training and scoring sessions, thus creating opportunities for them to develop a shared vision of teaching and to learn deeply about instruction.

> **Connecticut also raised standards for principals—and tied principals' training to their capacity to support and evaluate teachers.**

In the late 1990s, Connecticut infused the Interstate School Leadership Licensing Consortium (ISLLC) standards into preparation, licensure, and accreditation. In 2001, based on these standards, it created a performance assessment for school principals—the Connecticut Administrator Test (CAT)—which is used both to license principals and to inform accreditation for their preparation programs. The CAT poses authentic problems for potential principals focused on instructional leadership challenges: Among other things, candidates must show that they can accurately evaluate a teacher in response to his or her lesson plan, videotaped lesson, and samples of student work; provide useful feedback; and make a plan for professional development and support. They must also develop a school improvement plan for a school about which they receive extensive data concerning practices and outcomes.

In addition to the incentives the test provides for training programs to focus on teaching, learning, and school improvement—areas in which Connecticut principals feel better prepared than most in the country—each university is judged on its pass rates, and state accreditation depends, in part, on how well its candidates do on the test. If 80% or more do not pass, the university must redesign its program. Furthermore, because the assessment is evaluated by experienced Connecticut administrators and university faculty, who are trained for scoring, the assessment provides a powerful professional development opportunity for these other Connecticut professionals and a shared sense of standards of practice throughout the state.

In line with the expectations of the assessment, Connecticut principals are among the most likely nationwide to report that they feel well-prepared to evaluate teachers and provide instructional feedback, develop curriculum and instruction to support learning, and develop professional development. Principals we followed and observed in the study often focused on their efforts to provide learning opportunities for teachers. Typical of others was this description of planning for teacher support from a University of Connecticut graduate working as a principal in Hartford:

> The first course of business is to provide support for the teacher in whatever area I noticed the teacher is weak in. I may provide additional professional development elements, and that could take the form of going to a formal workshop or visiting another teacher's room who is successful in that area or me supporting the teacher myself, sitting down to brainstorm or come up with ideas that will support that teacher. I may even send a teacher to another school that is more successful in a specific curriculum initiative. I want to provide the teacher with as much support as possible.

> | **Principals engage teachers in goal-setting to guide practice and professional learning.** |
> | --- |

Principals also engage teachers in goal-setting to guide practice and professional learning. For example, another Hartford principal from the same program noted:

> We set an improvement plan each year as a school—it's a collaborative effort with the classroom teachers—and we set our assessments right in that plan so we have action steps and how we're going to evaluate them. . . . At the end of the year I have the staff members [look at] each of our action steps and how far they feel we progressed towards it, and then they comment on that as well. Then we meet as a staff to determine if that's a goal that needs to continue the following year with a different plan or if the plan should continue as it is, because there is some success noted.

These practices model what good evaluation is about and they create a context for ongoing analysis, growth, and development. In

> **In Connecticut, the state's continuum of development for teachers and its continuum of learning for principals are intertwined.**

Connecticut, the state's continuum of development for teachers and its continuum of learning for principals are intertwined, embedded in both credentialing systems and supported by professional development requirements, which creates a shared focus on and understanding of good teaching.

Specific Training in Teacher Evaluation and Supervision

As described in the previous chapter, the Teacher Advancement Program (TAP) has created a career ladder program that taps the skills of expert teachers for coaching and evaluation and trains them extensively for both roles. Both these lead teachers and principals who serve as evaluators are trained to rate teaching performance based on descriptive standards-based rubrics, which they learn to apply in sessions that use actual videotaped lessons. Each evaluator must be certified by demonstrating that he or she can rate teacher performance accurately—that is, within one point of benchmark scores from national raters on each indicator.

> **Lead teachers and principals who serve as evaluators are trained to rate teaching performance based on highly descriptive standards-based rubrics, which they learn to apply in sessions that use actual videotaped lessons.**

Evaluators are also trained in how to conduct post-conference sessions that can help teachers identify areas for improvement, and they must pass an assessment that certifies their ability to conduct these post-conferences well. Evaluators can receive ongoing training through Summer Institutes, and they are re-certified annually.

Together, the master teachers and principal comprise a leadership team for the schools. Among the many things the teams do to support instruction, they are trained to monitor inter-rater reliability in the evaluation system. They receive diagnostic reports, including scores by teacher and average scores for each standard and domain area by evaluator. These allow them to see whether some evaluators appear to be outliers in their scoring. Where this appears to be a problem, there are additional training resources that help evaluators build understanding of the rubric, including scoring exercises on specific standards, taped lessons, and access to outside certified evaluators, who can help them calibrate scores.[2]

It is important to note that this is more than a technical matter. As teachers and principals work to fine-tune their ability to look at teaching through a common lens, they are also building a shared understanding of practice and a greater capacity to support teaching collectively in ways that address the individual needs of students. As Lynn Gallagher, Master Teacher at Hilda Knoff Elementary School in Jefferson Parish, Louisiana, put it:

> **As teachers and principals work to fine-tune their ability to look at teaching through a common lens, they are also building a shared understanding of practice.**

> TAP allows teachers to make instructional decisions and implement instructional practices that meet the needs of teachers and their students. What TAP recognizes and values is the multifaceted, dynamic nature of instructional practice. Students (and teachers) are complex and varying in their needs—teaching and learning is not a one-size-fits-all! Unlike prepackaged and top-down instructional mandates that are handed down to teachers, TAP provides educators with the skills, knowledge, and resources to formulate practices that are effective and successful for the students being served.[3]

In Stanford's study of principal development programs, several districts had created extensive professional development centered on teacher supervision and evaluation for both principals and lead teachers. Three of the districts—Hartford, New York City's Region #1, and San Diego—used regular principals' conferences to anchor professional learning grounded in analyses of classroom practice. These are tied to school visits, coaching, and other supports for implementing new leadership practices, including those associated with successful supervision and development of teachers. One principal in Hartford described the integrated approach to evaluation and professional development he learned as part of the district's principal development strategy in this way:

I want [teachers] to feel used to me coming in to assess. Academic review is one of the ways [I support teachers] . . . monitoring the teacher's lesson plans that they submit to me each week, providing professional development for them that they're actually going to utilize, so there's not this disconnect where we go out to a conference somewhere and we come back and we never use what we were trained in. Then I monitor this through my observations.[4]

Learning how to integrate supervision with professional learning is a critical part of the training evaluators need.

Expert Teachers

Also important are the provision of supports for teachers who need additional assistance—something few principals have time to provide—and the creation of decision-making procedures and structures that allow personnel decisions to be made fairly and efficiently.

As I describe later in this chapter (see box: Peer Assistance and Review, pp. 124–125), this support comes in the form of Consulting Teachers, who are released full- or part-time from their regular teaching duties in order to coach other teachers who are identified as needing assistance. Consulting teachers are carefully selected for their teaching and leadership skills, and are trained to become expert mentors as well.

> **Also important are the provision of supports for teachers who need additional assistance and decision-making procedures and structures that allow personnel decisions to be made fairly and efficiently.**

Access to expert teachers who are given time for coaching is critical to an effective evaluation system. Because good practice is best developed *in* practice, rather than in workshops, and because intensive assistance for struggling teachers is best provided by content-area teachers who can support planning and instruction, being able to deploy teaching experts where they are needed is an important resource for principals to have available.

Rochester, New York, has undertaken innovative approaches to provide greater content expertise in the evaluation process and

> **Being able to deploy teaching experts where they are needed is an important resource for principals.**

to encourage teachers to work as—and be evaluated as—teams. There, teachers have the option to be observed and evaluated by a trained Lead Teacher/Peer Evaluator, if they so request, in addition to their administrative supervisor. Lead Teachers are selected by the Rochester Career In Teaching (CIT) Governing Panel, made up of six administrators appointed by the district and six teachers appointed by the teachers' union.

GOVERNANCE STRUCTURES THAT ENABLE PERSONNEL DECISIONS

Of course, an evaluation system based on standards of professional practice must also be able to remove individuals from the profession when they do not, after receiving assistance, meet professional standards. Peer Assistance and Review (PAR) programs have the most

> **An evaluation system must be able to remove individuals when they do not, after receiving assistance, meet professional standards.**
> **Peer Assistance and Review Programs—collaborations between unions and school boards—have proven more effective than traditional evaluation systems at both improving and efficiently dismissing teachers while avoiding union grievances.**

long-standing successful track record in accomplishing this goal. These programs rely on highly expert mentor teachers to provide assistance to beginning and veteran teachers who need support and to conduct some aspects of the evaluation process. The systems in Cincinnati, Columbus, and Toledo, Ohio; Rochester, New York; Poway and San Juan, California; and Seattle, Washington, have

all been studied and found successful in identifying teachers for continuation and tenure as well as those needing intensive assistance and personnel action.[5] These systems—collaborations between unions and school boards—which build in due process and assistance for teachers placed in intervention—have proven more effective than traditional evaluation systems at both improving and efficiently dismissing teachers while avoiding union grievances.

The PAR Governing Boards are critical to this process. A recent study of PAR programs noted that the boards ensure that solid evidence is brought to bear on personnel decisions and that the focus is on improving instruction. Furthermore,

> The Governance Boards turned out to be problem solving forums where district officials and union leaders collaboratively address routine operational and policy problems. . . . More than simple collaborative efforts, the partnerships developed through PAR enabled union and management together to make high-stakes decisions about teacher practice and evaluation.[6]

The decision-making process helps build a shared sense of responsibility and collaboration that extends into other areas of work, and helps union officials and district administrators maintain a focus on teaching and learning.

Key features of these systems thus include not only the instruments used for evaluation, but also the expertise of the consulting teachers or mentors—skilled teachers in the same subject areas and school levels, who have release time to serve as mentors—and a system of due process and review that involves a panel of teachers and administrators which makes recommendations about personnel decisions based on evidence from the evaluations. This joint committee oversees the work of the mentor teachers who support both beginning teachers prior to tenure and veteran teachers who are struggling. Based on reports from both the mentor teachers and the principals, the committee decides which teachers will receive tenure, which will have another year to improve, and

> **Mentor teachers support both beginning teachers prior to tenure and veteran teachers who are struggling.**

which will be dismissed. Similarly, the committee decides, before the school year is over, which teachers in the intervention program have improved sufficiently to be continued in the district.

PEER ASSISTANCE AND REVIEW

Peer Assistance and Review (PAR) programs have demonstrated over 30 years that it is possible to evaluate teachers rigorously, support them intensely, and make personnel decisions effectively. The first PAR program began in Toledo, Ohio, as a partnership between the school board and the teachers' union in the early 1980s. Union leader Dal Lawrence was convinced that "teaching would become a profession only when teachers, themselves, set standards for their work and decided who met those standards and deserved to teach."[7] To address these concerns, Lawrence proposed an intern program to the Toledo Public School District to better mentor and induct new teachers into the profession. The program also provides intensive support to veteran teachers who are struggling, and enables a timely and well-grounded decision to be made about tenure and continuation in the district.

Thirty years later, the Toledo PAR program has deepened and become the blueprint for other PAR programs across the country. Such programs now exist in at least 41 districts in 13 states (California, Colorado, Florida, Illinois, Indiana, Maryland, Michigan, Minnesota, Missouri, New Mexico, New York, Ohio, and Washington). A just-published study of PAR programs in California, where a state law encourages district adoption, documented the successes of the models in Poway and San Juan, California, demonstrating the capacity of the program to be successfully adapted to different contexts.[8]

How PAR Operates

In Toledo, the PAR governing body consists of an Internal Review Board made up of nine members (five teachers and four administrators) who oversee the program. Although the number of board members differs in other districts, panels generally include nearly equal numbers of teachers and administrators, with a slight edge to teacher members. This governing body is responsible for overseeing the work of the mentor teachers, as well as evaluating accumulated evidence on a participating teacher and making final tenure and employment recommendations to the superintendent of schools.

Selection of Consulting Teachers

Consulting Teachers, who provide the support and evaluation, have at least five years of teaching experience, and undergo an intensive selection process that includes classroom observations, interviews, a review of teaching evaluations, and recommendations from peers and administrators. In the

Toledo model, these mentors are employed full-time to support and evaluate approximately 10 novice and/or struggling teachers over the course of an individualized intervention or mentorship period. They serve no more than 3 years before returning to the classroom, and are paid an annual stipend of $5,000 to $7,000.

Support and Evaluation

Consulting Teachers design a support, intervention, and improvement plan based on the needs of each teacher. The support spans the five domains that comprise the evaluation criteria: planning and designing instruction, instruction, classroom management, assessment, and professional development. The specific tasks range from assistance with lesson planning and sharing of resources to observing classrooms and providing feedback on classroom management and instructional practices.

When working with experienced teachers, Consulting Teachers provide intensive guidance and direction, including helping them design and implement individualized improvement plans. Consulting Teachers make periodic reports to the Governance Board, marshaling accumulated evidence about each teacher's professional practice. At the conclusion of the teacher's time in PAR (usually a year), the Governance Board examines the Consulting Teacher's reports, the administrator's evaluations, and other evidence and makes a recommendation about whether or not the teacher should be retained in the district.

Program Effects

Studies of PAR outcomes have found that beginning teacher retention rates have increased significantly and that those who leave are now primarily those the district does not renew, rather than candidates who become disenchanted with teaching. On the national level, the National Center for Educational Statistics reports that the new-teacher attrition rate for those who participate in PAR programs is 15%, compared to 26% for those who do not.[9] Among intervention candidates, many improve; those who do not improve leave teaching without extended legal proceedings, because due process is built into the design of the model. A Harvard Graduate School of Education study of Toledo reports that nearly 8% of program participants from 1981 through 2008 were either dismissed or resigned after the first year of participation in PAR.[10]

In such systems, beginning teachers have been found to stay in teaching at higher rates because of the mentoring they receive, and those who leave are usually those the district has chosen not to continue rather than those who have quit. Among veteran teachers identified for assistance and review (usually 1% to 3% of the teaching force), many improve sufficiently to be removed from intervention status, and one-third to one-half leave by choice or by district request. Because teacher associations collaborate in creating and administering the programs, which are designed to ensure due process, there are no procedural grievances when a teacher is dismissed.

PEER ASSISTANCE AND REVIEW IN ACTION

To understand how such programs work in action, a team of researchers from Stanford Research International (SRI), working with J. Koppich & Associates, recently conducted an in-depth study of two California districts known for their well-developed PAR programs: Poway, an early California pioneer in this work, and San Juan, a district that built its program more recently.[11]

In the late 1980s, Don Raczka, a middle school mathematics teacher, and other teacher leaders from Poway studied Toledo's program and worked to bring its key features to their district. Like Toledo's, the Poway program was also designed to work with both novices and struggling teachers. As Poway has a long tradition of careful teacher selection, the primary goal was not to get rid of bad teachers, but to further develop good ones. At the same time, the program has effectively addressed the need for teacher accountability in the relatively rare cases where teachers do not become highly competent. Years later, Raczka, the now-retired president of the Poway Federation of Teachers, noted, "Today we have better trained teachers who are used to reflecting on their practice and talking about pedagogy. We want evaluation to make sense for them."[12]

In 1999, the California State Legislature authorized a statewide grant program for PAR programs, as part of a hybrid model designed to work in tandem with an existing induction program called Beginning Teacher Support Assessment (BTSA). This made California the first state to enact funding for this kind of teacher evaluation and mentoring strategy on a statewide basis. The San Juan district created its model with these funds. San Juan union leaders Tom Alves and Steve Duditch were strong supporters of the program after studying the work in Poway and other successful districts.

As in Toledo (and other PAR districts), San Juan and Poway use the program to sort out ineffective teachers who do not improve. Historically, about two-thirds of veterans identified for intervention have improved substantially and successfully completed the program; about one-third in each case resigned or were dismissed. Among beginning teachers, about 20% are not renewed as a result of the program. As the researchers noted, though, the effects of the program are much broader. For example, over the years, Poway's program for beginning teachers has served 1,875 individuals, more than 60% of the teachers currently in the district. Poway officials note that the success of the program in both building competence and weeding out poor performers at the beginning of their careers has helped to raise the overall quality of practice in the district. Both consulting teachers and those being mentored report that they became better teachers as a result of their careful analysis of and work on practice. Thus, there are relatively few teachers identified as struggling later in their careers.

Charlotte Kutzner, Program Coordinator for the Poway Professional Assistance Program (PPAP), explains how support and evaluation for beginning teachers are handled in this model, which has completely merged the traditional California program for beginning teachers (BTSA) with the PAR program for assisting veteran teachers. The program also combines the mentoring and evaluation functions that are sometimes kept separate in district evaluation systems:

> Poway's Professional Assistance Program is a BTSA program, and like others, we are responsible for meeting all of the induction standards [for beginning teachers]. But unlike most other induction programs, we are also responsible for evaluation of first-year teachers. So we observe and conference, we support teachers, but our evaluations are not confidential. When I work with a new teacher I share what I see in their classroom with their principal, and also report to a governance board, which includes the assistant superintendent of personnel, the union president, and two teachers. People ask, "How can you do both support and evaluation?" We do, and it has worked since 1987, and from the get-go it has

been evaluative. I would say that, over the years, 95% of the teachers I have worked with have forgotten that I am their evaluator by Thanksgiving. I am Charlotte, I am their friend, their colleague; I am there to support them.

There is also a program to support veteran teachers who have been rated as not meeting standards. This program, the Permanent Teacher Intervention Program (PTIP) [similar to PAR in other districts], is designed to assist permanent teachers who have been identified as being in serious professional jeopardy. The PTIP teacher receives assistance from a teacher consultant much like the new teacher does in the induction program. In this program, the principal remains the evaluator and the teacher consultant reports progress to the principal and the PPAP Governance Board. . . . Our program is successful because of our working relationship with the district and the union. This is truly a joint effort.[13]

Consulting teachers are carefully chosen by the Governance Board and the program director based on their teaching ability, coaching and communication skills, and leadership ability. In these districts, like many others with PAR programs, candidates submit evidence of their practice, leadership experience (including experience conducting professional development), and recommendations from colleagues and principals. In addition to review of these materials, and face-to-face interviews, they are observed teaching in their classrooms.

Applicants are selected into a pool of potential Consulting Teachers and are activated full- or part-time when a teacher with their content background and teaching level is needed. They can serve for 1 to 4 years before rotating back into the classroom. The Governance Board evaluates the work of the Consulting Teachers by reviewing their reports and presentations and can terminate a Consulting Teacher's appointment at any time if there are concerns about performance.

> **To learn this challenging job, the Consulting Teachers participate in their own professional development and regular problem-solving group with their peers.**

To learn this challenging job, the Consulting Teachers participate in their own professional development and regular problem-solving group with their peers, sharing ideas about how to address particular needs, have difficult conversations productively, and lasso the most appropriate resources for the cases they are working on.

In these districts, consulting teachers provide an extraordinary amount of support for instruction and evaluation, both for the teachers they work with directly and, often, for other teachers in the district as well. When working with teachers, they not only observe and give feedback, often videotaping or scripting the lessons so that there is a record of practice, they also work with participating teachers to develop lessons, assignments, classroom management systems, and grading systems; they help select and secure curriculum materials; they model lessons and analyze student work together; they may lead professional development events as well as attending them with participating teachers so that they can provide follow-up coaching; and they carefully and extensively document teachers' progress, both as a learning tool for the teacher and as part of the due process that accompanies evaluation.

As consulting teachers work with their charges, they develop a record that includes:

- a detailed improvement plan;
- detailed logs of each observation and conference with the participating teacher;
- meeting notes, email correspondence, sample lesson plans, and other supporting evidence; and
- summary reports the Consulting Teachers produce every 2 months for the Governance Board.

The amount of care they can take with this process—and the investment they are able to make—is revealed by the SRI analysis of their contribution to the support and evaluation process. Whereas principals averaged 1 formal evaluation and 2 informal evaluations of the teachers referred to PAR in an academic year, Consulting Teachers averaged 5 formal evaluations and 38 informal observations in which they offered intensive assistance and mentoring. And where principals' records of their observations, assistance, and participating teachers' progress averaged 7 pages in a year, those of the Consulting Teachers averaged 190. These records detail the focus on improving teachers' practice as much as documenting their strengths and weaknesses. They are a record for advice and counsel and the source of the Governance Board's later review.

The end result of this investment is that most teachers who are placed in intervention under PAR improve considerably (see box: A Snapshot of One Teacher's Progress Under PAR, for an illustrative case). Meanwhile, those who do not improve either leave on their own or are dismissed without grievances, because teachers are clear about their practice in relation to the standards for teaching and about the due process they have experienced. As the California research team noted:

> The end result of this investment is that most teachers who are placed in intervention under PAR improve considerably. Meanwhile, those who do not improve either leave on their own or are dismissed without grievances.

> PAR sets a higher bar for performance review than conventional teacher evaluation. . . . The intensive support and multidimensional evaluation have shown that the teacher is ready to be responsible for a classroom or have provided ample evidence that he or she is not. . . . PAR accomplishes what traditional evaluation does not. It gives teachers ample and supported opportunity to improve their practice and be successful. For those who do not or cannot improve, the performance documentation generated through PAR offers what San Juan union president Steve Duditch called "an airtight case"—evidence so compelling that the action that needs to be taken is clear.[14]

A SNAPSHOT OF ONE TEACHER'S PROGRESS UNDER PAR

Elizabeth, a fifth-grade teacher referred into PAR, successfully completed the PAR program after a full academic year of intensive work with her Consulting Teacher, Amanda. Amanda worked directly with Elizabeth for at least 88 hours over the course of the year. Their work together included at least 52 informal observations (averaging 1–2 per week), frequent conferences about challenges and next steps, and in-depth collaboration on issues such as classroom organization, instructional strategies, and lesson planning (including joint meetings with Elizabeth's principal to clarify expectations for lesson plans). Amanda also modeled lessons in Elizabeth's classroom for at least 1 full day and 4 half-days over the course of the academic year.

Elizabeth's progress toward meeting the two standards for which she was referred into PAR appeared relatively slow at first. During each of the first two of the five reporting periods for the PAR panel, Amanda's formal evaluations of Elizabeth revealed that she was meeting only one of five elements related to engaging and supporting all students in learning (Standard 1) and one of six elements related to maintaining effective environments for student learning (Standard 2).

Early on, Amanda determined that if Elizabeth were to meet the standards, she would need to include strategies to improve the physical organization and environment of the classroom, strategies to consistently monitor and manage student behavior and to keep students on task, strategies to use teaching time effectively, and strategies to differentiate instruction and provide deeper, more reflective learning opportunities for students. Rather than address all these strategies simultaneously, Amanda focused on one strategy at a time. For example, during their early work together, Amanda spent substantial time on Elizabeth's physical classroom environment, suggesting changes to remove some barriers to student engagement, and showing Elizabeth that those changes made students easier to manage and more attentive. With this early change, Amanda was able to help Elizabeth see her own progress and made it easier for Elizabeth to see that many of her students were "quietly disengaged." This enabled Elizabeth to try new instructional strategies. Over time, Amanda built on this foundation to help Elizabeth see that the newly expanded range of instructional strategies she was using were better engaging her students.

The notes from these two observation periods revealed that Amanda had been guiding Elizabeth toward steady progress in understanding and addressing the barriers to effective instruction and student learning, setting Elizabeth up for more rapid progress as the year went on. By the end of the third reporting period, Amanda found that Elizabeth was meeting all but two elements of Standard 1 and all but one element of Standard 2. By the fourth reporting period, Elizabeth was consistently and successfully meeting all elements of these standards. Elizabeth continued to meet all elements in the fifth reporting period, and Amanda focused her support on helping Elizabeth maintain consistency and independently sustain these improvements.

Source: Humphrey, Koppich, Bland, & Bosetti (2012).

A FEASIBLE SYSTEM THAT IS ADEQUATELY RESOURCED

A final requirement of a productive evaluation system is that it be feasible to implement well—on the part of both the evaluators and those being evaluated—and that it be adequately resourced to be effective. These conditions have been a challenge to achieve, especially in the rush to construct complex new systems under the requirements of the federal Race to the Top initiatives and the new Elementary and Secondary Education Act (ESEA) flexibility waivers, both of which create complicated mandates for teacher evaluation systems.

Three major issues require attention:

- The adequacy of human resources to implement the system,
- The sustainability of the system balanced with other aspects of school operations, and
- The appropriateness and manageability of the measures of teaching.

The Adequacy of Human Resources

One of the historical failings of teacher evaluation systems in the United States has been their typical reliance on the school principal alone as the person expected to observe teachers, mentor those who are beginners, coach those who need help, document concerns and support processes for those who are struggling, and make the final call on whether to recommend dismissal, based on the record that has been assembled. Principals also have to handle dozens of other academic and nonacademic obligations to boards, central offices, teachers, parents, and students daily. Furthermore, in high-poverty settings, they have many social services and categorical programs to juggle so that children will be fed, housed, protected, and receive health care.

> One of the historical failings of teacher evaluation systems has been their typical reliance on the school principal alone as the person expected to observe, mentor, coach, document, and make the final call on dismissal.

Unlike systems in some other countries, which have an additional administrative role for handling the nonacademic side of schooling (e.g., buses, business matters, and so on), American principals are typically expected to do it all. It is easy to see how attention to teacher support and evaluation can become difficult under these circumstances. And in larger schools, where there may be as many as 100 teachers, it is impossible for intensive evaluations to be conducted for every teacher every year by a lone school principal. (In business settings, for example, the appropriate span of control is generally considered to be one supervisor to seven employees, at most.)

> **In business settings, the appropriate span of control is generally considered to be one supervisor to seven employees.**

As we have seen, consulting teachers are among the most important resources offered for evaluation in PAR systems, just as master and mentor teachers supplement the principal's efforts in schools that use the TAP program and in other districts that have developed career ladders. These expert resources are a key element of teaching support in high-performing systems like Singapore's as well. In large schools, especially, having teachers who bring content expertise, mentoring skill, and time to the task of supporting and assessing novices and other teachers who need assistance is a necessary component of an evaluation system that can successfully support improvement and personnel decision making.

Teacher leaders working with the Center for Teaching Quality point out additional benefits of peer evaluation:

> Finally, we argue that a key to strengthening [teacher evaluation] will be to involve more classroom teachers in the process of reviewing their colleagues. We make this claim for several reasons: One is that good teachers know content and how to teach it—and this component needs to be a part of an improved [evaluation program]. The second is that administrators are overburdened with many complex issues that only they can address. Schools are not funded and organized to support a more rigorous and in-depth teacher evaluation system. The third is that any effective teacher

evaluation system will need to be closely connected to other elements of teacher development from pre-service, induction and professional development in working communities of teaching professionals.[15]

The Sustainability of the System

Districts that have successfully resolved the tension between the need for high-quality evaluation and principal time have typically included assistant principals, department chairs, and master or mentor teachers in the evaluation process. In addition, they have often created a cycle of more intensive evaluations in periodic years (for example, once every 2 or 3 years) for veteran teachers who have been previously well rated, so as to provide more time for those teachers who need attention. In the nonsummative years, teachers in good standing continue to engage in goal-setting and professional learning (see Chapter 5, for example), but the burden on their administrators is lower.

> **Districts that have successfully resolved the tension between the need for high-quality evaluation and principal time have typically included assistant principals, department chairs, and master or mentor teachers in the evaluation process.**

In particular, if leaders are to support and evaluate beginners intensively and make well-grounded decisions at the point of tenure, and if they are to focus on the needs of teachers who are not succeeding and make appropriate personnel decisions about continuation, they must have the freedom to use their limited time wisely.

Furthermore, much of the work to improve teaching quality occurs outside of the boundaries of individual teacher evaluation, as principals and teacher leaders work to guide collaboration and inquiry within professional learning communities, to shape professional development activities, to enable collective curriculum planning, and to support peer coaching. When these activities are ignored, it is very difficult to move the needle on the improvement of practice in a school. For busy educators, finding the right balance in investing time and energy where it will pay off is critical to supporting school improvement and student learning.

This lesson has sometimes been ignored as teacher evaluation practices have been mandated by policymakers who live far from schools. For example, in Tennessee, one of the first states to mandate a Race to the Top evaluation system, the legislature required in 2010 that half of a teacher's evaluation be based on annual observations and half on student achievement data. In a bizarre twist on the notion of accountability, teachers in untested subjects and grade levels must choose the scores of another teacher to count for their evaluation. In 2011, the state board of education ruled that, each year, evaluators would conduct formal observations of all new teachers six times, and all tenured ones four times, scoring them in a computerized system that includes a total of 116 subcategories. Principals report that between the pre-conference, the observation itself, the post-conference, and several hours inputting data, they can spend the equivalent of a full day evaluating a single teacher.

Veteran middle school principal Will Shelton, who has routinely visited every classroom in his building several times a week, says that the new system has undermined rather than enhanced his ability to evaluate teaching by requiring him to spend so much time filling out paperwork that he cannot get out to classrooms nearly as often. Shortly after the system was launched, he noted:

> I've never seen such nonsense . . . In the five years I've been principal here, I've never known so little about what's going on in my own building. [The requirement that excellent veteran teachers be observed as often as new or weak ones] . . . is an insult to my best teachers, but it's also a terrible waste of time.[16]

> **New [Tennessee] evaluation policies "put everyone under stress, are divisive, and suck the joy out of a building."**

Shelton argued that between the test-based requirements and the excessive observation requirements, the new state evaluation policies "put everyone under stress, are divisive, and suck the joy out of a building."[17] Another Tennessee high school principal, Troy Kilzer, noted:

> It's one thing to be observing—I love that, it's my primary role. . . . But you know a good lesson is being taught without looking at a rubric. . . . We are spending a lot of time evaluating people we know are very good teachers.[18]

To the state's credit, Tennessee has begun to make alterations in the evaluation system, allowing the data to be collected in fewer visits, for example. Without a sensible approach to designing feasible evaluation systems, the opportunity costs could outweigh the benefits. The costs for principals are in time that could be spent in other classrooms, working with parents and families, and organizing collaborative work among teachers. The costs for a school may be that the joint efforts to build a positive school culture and a coherent curriculum are neglected, despite the fact that these are essential to actually improving teaching effectiveness.

Researchers who examined the pilot implementation of a similar system of evaluation in Los Angeles Unified School District (LAUSD) observed some of the same kinds of challenges, documenting many administrators and teachers who felt overwhelmed by the number of visits, the demands of documentation, and the need to coordinate multiple observers. As one administrator remarked of the process of working with two teachers who were part of the pilot:

> It's extremely challenging because, first of all, we don't have enough resources on site. . . . And so, when you go in and you have to really dedicate time to observing and transcribing, and going back and tagging the work, it's very time-consuming . . . I have two people [teachers] on site who are doing this, going through this process. Each one has a different second observer. So, I have to coordinate. . . . So, that in and of itself is a huge obstacle.[19]

And a pilot teacher commented:

> I have a family. [I'm] married with kids, so the time that it takes to . . . really sit . . . and do this. . . . It's not feasible, to be honest with you. The detail in what they want us to describe certain tasks or lesson plans we have. . . . I had no problem doing that in college because I was in college, but now I'm working. I've got to do lesson plans. I've got a wife, kids. . . . A couple of hours a weekend [is all I have] to do this.[20]

Fortunately, the LAUSD decided to pilot the system in order to collect data, fine-tune the requirements, and train teachers and administrators more fully, before taking it district-wide. This wise decision, called "initiative-saving" by a district leader, is one that states and districts should consider following.

The Appropriateness of Teaching Measures

A final area of concern has been whether the measures of teaching are appropriate and manageable. As noted earlier, in some systems, the desire to capture every aspect of teaching has led to systems that require reams of paperwork to address rubrics that are dozens of pages long, and documentation that takes many hours to complete. This can render systems infeasible over the long haul, especially if they take excessive time away from the primary work of schools: serving students, connecting with their families, and improving teaching and learning.

> The desire to capture every aspect of teaching has led to systems that require reams of paperwork to address rubrics that are dozens of pages long.

More troubling are behavioral measurement systems that fail to understand that teaching is more than implementing a set of canned routines in each lesson. If teachers are to be effective, the tactics used must be chosen in relation to particular teaching goals at particular moments for particular students. When effective teachers are building on students' prior knowledge, engaging them in the subject matter, and enabling them to apply their knowledge, they will use a wide range of tools when they are most useful: direct instruction and investigation, lectures and group work, tightly structured assignments and more open-ended projects, writing and in-class discussions, and so on.

Unfortunately, some behaviorist instruments fail to understand or examine how teachers choose their strategies in relation to the teaching goals and standards. This was a prominent problem in checklists that were built into evaluation systems decades ago. I remember, for example, when a Florida teacher of the year in the late 1980s did not pass muster on that state's evaluation system, because he was rated down for answering a question with another question, a method that Socrates used all the time.[21] That instrument also checked to be sure that teachers were keeping a "brisk pace of instruction," offering particular kinds of praise to students, and structuring their lessons in particular ways, without concern for whether these strategies were working for students.

Such checklist approaches not only assume, wrongly, that the same tactics are needed for all teaching goals and all students, they also fail to take into account the nature of teaching cycles: that teachers use different strategies to pursue different goals at different moments in time. For example, teachers will engage students in different kinds of activities when they are first introducing a topic, when they are in the midst of a project or activity, when they are providing feedback, when they are encouraging revisions or re-teaching certain concepts, and so on. This kind of problem has recently surfaced in the early implementation of several evaluation systems, including the new Tennessee teacher evaluation system. One account described the problem from the perspective of Nashville principal Steve Ball, who had just finished observing a 60-minute English class where the teacher was introducing the concept of irony:

> "It was a good lesson," Mr. Ball said. But under Tennessee's new teacher-evaluation system, which is similar to systems being adopted around the country, Mr. Ball said he had to give the teacher a one—the lowest rating on a five-point scale—in one of 12 categories: breaking students into groups. Even though Mr. Ball had seen the same teacher, a successful veteran he declined to identify, group students effectively on other occasions, he felt that he had no choice but to follow the strict guidelines of the state's complicated rubric. "It's not an accurate reflection of her as a teacher," Mr. Ball said.[22]

Teacher association leader Gera Summerford compared the evaluation system to "taking your car to the mechanic and making him use all of his tools to fix it, regardless of the problem, and expecting him to do it in an hour."[23] The IMPACT system used in Washington, D.C., has been criticized for the same problem. Under IMPACT, teachers receive five 30-minute classroom observations in which they are expected to demonstrate 22 distinctly different teaching elements in nine categories, regardless of what they are trying to accomplish in that period of time.[24] Middle school teacher and mentor Ellen Berg described a similar checklist system once in effect in San Diego, California:

> Because there is not a common language about what quality teaching is, in some cases we use a checklist of random things. In San Diego Unified they had us go visit classrooms with a list of all these things that

were supposed to be going on—group-work, cooperative learning, etc. It was impossible to do all these things in a 15- (or even 50-) minute period, and teachers were being ripped up for not doing everything on the list.[25]

As we have seen in previous eras of reform, in systems like these, teachers begin designing lessons to meet the checklist, rather than to accomplish their goals with students. In such cases, teacher evaluation can work against good teaching, rather than for it. Ironically, overly prescriptive evaluation systems like these can lead to the triumph of technique over purpose, and may ultimately undermine rather than enhance teachers' effectiveness.

Prescriptive checklists, which are based on a partial, flawed understanding of teaching as the implementation of unvarying routines, differ from standards-based evaluation tools that look at broader patterns of teaching practice in relation to teaching goals. They are generally adopted to reduce the need for judgment on the part of the evaluator, in the mistaken belief that objective tallies can substitute for a deeper appreciation of good teaching, which can only be properly understood in a reciprocal relationship with student needs and student learning.

> **Standards-based evaluation tools look at broader patterns of teaching practice in relation to teaching goals.**

These approaches cannot ultimately succeed at the goal of building a more effective teaching force. At the end of the day, professional teaching—like practice in all other professions—must rest on expert judgments about how to meet the nonstandardized needs of clients using a wide repertoire of strategies appropriately. It is critical that teacher evaluation be helpful in this quest, rather than an obstacle or impediment to good practice on the part of principals or teachers.

> **It is critical that teacher evaluation be helpful, rather than an obstacle or impediment to good practice on the part of principals or teachers.**

The Need for a Strategic Approach

In any business, it is problematic for the evaluation of the work to become so mechanical or cumbersome that it gets in the way of productivity and the actual conduct of the work. To avoid this outcome, designers of evaluation processes should consider how to create a sensible, feasible strategy by:

- Ensuring that instruments capture teaching authentically and succinctly, without an excessive number of indicators or behaviors to be tallied, and with respect for the relationship between teaching decisions, teaching goals, and student needs;
- Providing resources for the evaluation process in the form of expert teachers who can undertake some aspects of the evaluation process and provide intensive assistance where it is needed;
- Focusing evaluation resources especially on key needs: support for beginning teachers and teachers experiencing difficulty in the classroom, and the documentation needed for fair, effective decisions about tenure and continuation in those cases;
- Creating processes by which veteran teachers in good standing can alternate years in which they experience more intensive summative evaluation with years in which they engage in formative evaluation organized around goal-setting and professional learning.

It is easy for procedures to overwhelm purpose in almost any reform, and this is particularly true for evaluation. As states and districts develop new approaches, it will be important for them to think strategically about how to accomplish their goals—putting in place the necessary systems and supports that allow educators to focus productively on improving teaching. As new practices are implemented, districts will also need to study and refine them, always mindful of keeping

> **It is easy for procedures to overwhelm purpose in almost any reform, and this is particularly true for evaluation.**

their eyes on the prize: more responsive and effective teaching in each classroom and across the school as a whole.

8 Remember the Goal: Keep Your Eyes on the Prize

> Comprehensive evaluations—with standards and scoring rubrics and multiple classroom observations . . . and a role for student work and teacher reflections—are valuable regardless of the degree to which they predict student achievement, and regardless of whether they're used to weed out a few bad teachers or a lot of them. They contribute much more to the improvement of teaching than today's drive-by evaluations or test scores alone. And they contribute to a much more professional atmosphere in schools. As a result, they make public school teaching more attractive to the sort of talent that the occupation has struggled to recruit and retain. Capable people want to work in environments where they sense they matter. . . . Comprehensive evaluation systems send a message that teachers are professionals doing important work.
>
> —Thomas Toch & Robert Rothman (2008)[1]

Many initiatives to measure and improve teaching effectiveness through evaluation have emerged as pressures for improved student achievement have intensified. Such initiatives will have the greatest payoff if they stimulate practices known to support student learning and are embedded in systems that also *develop* greater teaching competence. Such systems will be based on professional teaching standards and instruction focused on meaningful curriculum content. They will make intense use of coaching and offer extensive opportunities for teachers to help their colleagues and their schools improve. Policies that create increasingly valid measures of teaching effectiveness—and that create innovative systems for recognizing, developing, and utilizing expert teachers—can ultimately help to create a more effective teaching profession.

> **Policies that create increasingly valid measures of teaching effectiveness can ultimately help to create a more effective teaching profession.**

Although there is potential for improving teaching through a coherent, high-quality system for teacher evaluation, there is also, as we have seen, potential for harm in a system that relies on invalid tools or ill-considered processes for evaluation. Evaluation should support teaching and teacher learning that enable greater effectiveness for both individuals and groups of teachers. It should support rather than deflect attention from the goal of school-wide improvement. And it should make teaching more rewarding and attractive, rather than driving talented people away from the profession.

> **Although there is potential for improving teaching through a coherent, high-quality system for teacher evaluation, there is also, as we have seen, potential for harm in a system that relies on invalid tools or ill-considered processes.**

To create systems that achieve these goals, this book has outlined several critical elements. These address not only evaluation instruments or procedures, but also the policy systems in which they operate and the school-based conditions that are needed to stimulate continuous learning and improvement. Important conditions include:

- **Clear professional standards** against which teachers are assessed both for state licensing and for on-the-job evaluation;
- **A continuum of performance assessments** that validly and reliably measure actual teaching performance at key career junctures—initial licensing, the achievement of the professional license, and the designation of accomplished practice;
- On-the-job evaluations that evaluate teacher effectiveness based on **multiple measures**, including
   → *evaluation of practice* based on classroom observations and examination of other classroom evidence (e.g., lesson plans, student assignments and work samples) using a **standards-based** instrument that examines planning, instruction, the learning environment, and student assessment;
   → *evidence of learning* by the teacher's students on a **range of valid assessments** that appropriately evaluate the curriculum and the students the teacher teaches, including students with special education needs and English language learners; and

→ *evaluation of teachers' contributions to colleagues* and to the school as a whole.
- Connected, ongoing, **high-quality professional learning** opportunities that build strong professional learning communities and enable teachers to meet the standards;
- **Structures that enable fair, effective evaluation** by ensuring evaluator training, expert teachers who can providing intensive assistance to teachers in need, governance structures that oversee the process and make timely, well-grounded personnel decisions, and resources that can support a manageable system; and
- **Teacher participation** in developing the system and in the governance structure that supports the ongoing decision-making processes.

Where these elements are in place, the evaluation experience can support the development of sophisticated teaching. (See box: Evaluation That Identifies Quality and Promotes Teacher Learning, which expresses the vision of a group of accomplished teachers for what evaluation should become.)

EVALUATION THAT IDENTIFIES QUALITY AND PROMOTES TEACHER LEARNING

Louisa, a fourth-year science teacher, sits down to discuss her teacher development portfolio with her evaluator. Her portfolio by now contains documentation and analysis of her work from the end of her preservice program through her first 3 years in the classroom. It also contains records and assessments of professional development projects she has done over the last 3 years. Louisa and her evaluators had selected these at different times in her first years of teaching to help her attend to the needs they identified together.

Susannah, who is Louisa's current evaluator, is a 15-year veteran science teacher at the same school. She is released to work as a member of the district evaluation team for three periods each day. In that role, Susannah observes her colleagues, prepares written evaluations, meets with teachers to discuss or plan observations, and attends meetings where the district team reviews evaluations and individual professional development plans. The district evaluation

(Continued)

team is composed of accomplished classroom teachers, administrators from each school site, and the district Peer Assistance and Review coordinator. Their job is to review the evaluations of teachers to ensure that each of them is meeting performance expectations, progressing along the teacher development continuum, and receiving good counsel about ways to improve performance. When there are cases of serious concern about a teacher's performance, the team sends in another evaluator to validate the concern and help the team recommend a course of action that may range from targeted coaching to dismissal.

Louisa opens her observation notebook to the page that contains notes about the lesson that Susannah observed the previous day. Susannah has already given Louisa a copy of the observation notes she made and questions for her to think about before they meet. Louisa has added some reflections about the lesson and questions she wants to explore with Susannah. Louisa has brought some writing her students did that morning in response to a question she posed when they came into class. Susannah asks Louisa for her own assessment of the lesson and, in particular, how well she thinks that the discussions went. Louisa is very proud of the fact that during the discussion, she had to interject clarifying questions only three times. She points to evidence in the discussion of the content mastery students showed. However, there is a discrepancy between what occurred during the discussion and evidence of content mastery in the students' writing that Louisa has brought along.

In her observation notes, Susannah cites many of the same kinds of evidence that Louisa has discussed. She points out that the students still struggle to explain their thinking clearly. She directs Louisa's attention to the students' use of questions to one another and their limited reference to the informational texts they had read. This is an "ah-hah moment" for Louisa.

"Oh," she says, "this is what we've talked about when we have been trying to figure out why the kids do poorly on comprehension questions on informational texts!" She is referring to the meeting they had after they had looked at some of the school's standardized test data alongside other assessments. Louisa had complained several times about how few questions her students asked about their reading and how literal their conversations about their reading often were. She suggested that students' lack of questions might well be related to their ability to pose questions about the text as they read.

Susannah reminds Louisa that inquiry in science means being able to ask "why?" at the appropriate times. Louisa knows this and recognizes that posing questions while reading is a way readers probe their own understanding. If students were not doing that during reading, then very likely they would not notice that their own written or verbal explanations did not offer the receiver opportunities for clear understanding. "What should I do about this?" Louisa asks.

Susannah suggests that Louisa and her colleagues, who have been doing some action research on students' reading in science, invite one of the English teachers who has taught reading to English learners for several years to come to their next research meeting to help them explore strategies to try with these students.

Susannah's role will be to focus her observations on helping Louisa reflect on the success of the strategies she uses. As Susannah looks for evidence of teaching standards in Louisa's work this year, they agree she will focus on the effective teaching skills that she brings to solving this problem. They conclude by filing the observations, the records of their conversations, and agreements in the year 4 section of Louisa's portfolio. Thus begins a new chapter in Louisa's documentation of her professional journey.

Source: Accomplished California Teachers (2012).

For this kind of seamless and supportive evaluation system to operate, several particularly important aspects of a comprehensive system must be achieved. These include:

- Coordination of the state licensing system with local evaluation;
- Integration of evidence about teachers' practice with appropriate evidence about student learning; and
- Connection of evaluation with individual and collective professional learning.

COORDINATING STATE LICENSING AND LOCAL EVALUATION

One of the reasons for current concerns about the capability of some members of the teaching force is the public perception that teacher education and licensing systems do not routinely guarantee competence when teachers enter the profession. Furthermore, there is a large disjuncture in most states between the standards that are used to guide preparation and licensing and those that come into play when teachers are working on the job.

Fixing these problems is critical to developing a strong teaching profession. A profession is defined by the fact that all entrants have mastered a common body of knowledge and skills, which

> **A profession is defined by the fact that all entrants have mastered a common body of knowledge and skills, which is grounded in research, reflected in professional standards, and used to advance clients' welfare.**

is grounded in research, reflected in professional standards, and used to advance clients' welfare. Professions enforce these standards through professional licensing examinations that measure the capacity to apply knowledge responsibly—such as the bar exam in law, medical licensing examinations, and the portfolios required for architectural registration.

Like the new teacher performance assessments described in Chapters 2 and 3 of this book, these professional licensing and certification assessments are administered outside of the context of preparation or employment, so that they represent the knowledge and skills of the field as a whole, not just the views of a particular institution. They are scored by professionals who are trained to a common standard. These assessments also exert influence over preparation programs, because they help define the curriculum to be taught as they instantiate many of the knowledge and skills candidates are supposed to learn. In the employment context, local institutions, such as hospitals, law firms, and architectural firms, make the judgments of competence, but they use the standards of the profession as a whole to establish whether professionals have engaged in appropriate practice or malpractice.

Because teacher licensing tests, which are focused largely on basic skills and subject-matter knowledge, have not provided a meaningful assessment of capacity to teach before entry, teaching has lacked this key element of a profession. The lack of a meaningful entry bar also means that the burden has fallen on school districts to figure out whether new teachers have mastered the basics they should be bringing with them to the classroom. In teaching, it is time to create performance-based assessments for licensure and then to apply the same professional standards to local evaluation. The INTASC standards, adopted by more than 40 states, undergird new performance-based assessments for entry that have been developed by teachers and teacher educators—and a growing number of states are now beginning to use them to shape local evaluation instruments.

Louisa's case described earlier illustrates the learning that such a coordinated system could produce. As a fourth-year teacher,

Louisa has been developing her skills and documenting her practice around the same teaching standards from her preservice program throughout her first 3 years in the classroom. The portfolio she has maintained began with the performance assessment she completed at the end of preservice preparation to illustrate her ability to plan, teach, and assess students around the state student learning standards—and to reflect on her practice and outcomes in light of the state's standards for teaching.

This seamless experience was facilitated by an overhaul of the state system to require a teacher performance assessment for licensing, raising the bar for entry with a valid and authentic measure of whether new entrants can practice responsibly. The assessment (in this case, the Performance Assessment for California Teachers) is based on the same teaching standards that are used to accredit Louisa's preparation program, so her training was organized to ensure that she would master the tested knowledge and skills. The assessment helped strengthen her preparation and her readiness to teach. The coherence of her experience was further enabled by the extension of these standards into her induction program and later on-the-job evaluation.

> **Creating coherence from preparation to practice will greatly improve the capacity of the teaching force.**

Creating coherence from preparation to practice will greatly improve the capacity of the teaching force. States such as Massachusetts, Minnesota, Ohio, and Washington are among those that have taken steps forward to create such coherence, by adopting performance assessments for licensing beginning teachers, linked to standards for initial induction and ongoing evaluation. The role of the state—to establish professional standards and ensure, through profession-wide assessments for licensing, that all new entrants meet them—should complement the role of local districts, making it more possible for them to support the ongoing development of teachers who have met that initial bar.

INTEGRATING EVIDENCE OF PRACTICE WITH EVIDENCE OF STUDENT LEARNING

Louisa's case also illustrates how the evaluation process can connect evidence of practice to evidence of student learning in ways that move teaching forward. By looking at standardized test data, Louisa's department highlighted some areas for further exploration that might better support achievement. By looking, then, at authentic student work in the context of her current teaching, Louisa was able, with help from her evaluator, to see more clearly how her students were thinking and understanding, and to fine-tune her plans to strengthen their learning.

As Chapters 4 and 5 demonstrated, integrating authentic, rich evidence of student learning with the processes of evaluation—at the stage of goal-setting, throughout the course of the year, and at the end of teaching cycles (a year, a semester, or a unit of study)—can help teachers, mentors, and evaluators see first-hand what students know and can do before, during, and as a result of teaching. This evidence is directly associated with the curriculum and teaching goals, and it can include vivid examples of student thinking, reasoning, and performance on a wide range of knowledge and skills.

> **Evaluation systems that rely on a single test-based metric sitting in isolation alongside a rating based on classroom observations are not particularly helpful and can be harmful.**

Although standardized test scores can give a general idea of the level of student achievement (typically limited to items that ask for recognition of information), the scores they report do not offer detailed insights into what students think or what they know how to do in practice. The scores that result from most current state tests are limited by the inability of the tests to assess achievement that requires communication, research, the production of new ideas or products, or the application of knowledge to new problems or situations. In addition, as described in Chapter 5, value-added measures based on these tests, which are not designed to measure achievement that is well above or below grade level, are both unstable and biased for teachers who serve certain groups of students. Finally, it is nearly impossible to attribute student gains in test scores to a single teacher or to disentangle them from the many other influences on student learning, as well as the composition of the classroom.

Thus, evaluation systems that rely on a single test-based metric sitting in isolation alongside a rating based on classroom observations are not particularly helpful in either understanding or improving the quality of teaching and may be harmful. Quite often, the two measures do not agree with one another, and the variations in the value-added metric are unrelated to any specific changes in teaching practice. A single test measure used for all teachers may also be invalid for particular students or a poor measure of the specific curriculum being taught.

To be useful, measures of teaching outcomes must be considered in a more nuanced analysis that is connected to the curriculum and students being taught, as well as to the practice of the teacher being evaluated. These measures may include test scores of various kinds, with greater weight placed on those that are the most direct measures of the content being studied and on those that are most appropriate for the students in the classroom. Measures should also include student work that is drawn from specific undertakings in the classroom that can be analyzed in terms of teachers' practices focused on particular learning goals. As described in Chapters 4 and 5, this kind of work can be used to closely evaluate the teaching–learning cycle and transform how teachers think about and enact their practice.

A recent study from the Consortium on Policy Research in Education (CPRE) describes the importance of connecting information on teacher practice to information on student learning. The study looked at whether instruction and student outcomes would be influenced by having teachers discuss evidence about their practice, derived from classroom observations, along with student learning data. Compared with a control group of teachers who only discussed student data, the group that received feedback about their teaching in the same sessions where they discussed student learning data with colleagues exhibited more changes in their later instructional strategies of the kind emphasized in the feedback, and their students experienced significantly greater learning gains.[2]

Although it may seem simpler in the short run to make teacher decisions based largely on a single set of student scores, it is clear that this approach has thus far produced more heat than light in analyses of teaching, often creating greater confusion where more clarity is needed. Unskilled use

> **The greatest benefits will be secured where multiple measures of learning are combined with evidence of practice.**

of this kind of test score data can have damaging ramifications due to the mis-evaluation and potential loss of good teachers and the incentives for teachers to avoid the neediest students. Although attention to learning outcomes is important, the greatest benefits will be secured where multiple measures of learning are combined with evidence of practice to paint a meaningful picture of how teaching influences student growth and progress.

> **The goal is not merely to rank teachers on a single scale. It is to support quality instruction for all students.**

In this aspect of evaluation, especially, it is important to keep our eyes on the prize: Our goal is not merely to rank teachers on a single scale. It is to support quality instruction for all students—instruction that is well informed by a sophisticated understanding of what students are learning and how teaching can support their progress.

THE CRITICAL IMPORTANCE OF A COLLECTIVE PERSPECTIVE

Throughout this book, I have stressed the fact that teaching improves most in collegial settings where common goals are set, curriculum is jointly developed, and expertise is shared. In fact, research shows that student gains are most pronounced where teachers have greater longevity and work as a team. Although individual teacher evaluation can be a part of an educational improvement strategy, it cannot substitute for ongoing investments in the development and dissemination of profession-wide knowledge through preservice preparation and work in professional learning communities.

> **Research shows that student gains are most pronounced where teachers have greater longevity and work as a team.**

One more example may best serve to make this point. Lynne Formigli, a National Board Certified teacher in science, and a leader in her local union, describes how participating in the alternative evaluation program in Santa Clara Unified School District helped her address her goals concerning improving student writing, and learn much more in the process:

> In my continuing struggle to improve student writing, I teamed up with a 7th- and 8th-grade writing teacher. Our focus was on how we teach

writing at different grade levels. We each spent time observing each other teaching the writing process. Afterwards, we met and compared our observations. We came away with specific ways to improve our students' writing, as well as ideas for integrating writing throughout all grade levels and subjects. Observing other teachers demonstrating the writing process to their students helped me understand how critically important modeling is, allowing me to overcome my fear of giving students the answers when I give them examples. We found that in our search to help students be more effective communicators, we had all developed similar tools to scaffold their writing. During our discussions we were excited to consider the impact on our students if we standardized the tools we use, so students would recognize them from class to class, grade level to grade level. As we continue to work toward that goal as a school, we have the added benefit of increased communication and collaboration among teachers. The end result is of great benefit to the students we teach every day.[3]

Lynne's principal also learned from the experience. After Lynne and her two colleagues presented a summary of their work and a reflection on the process, he wrote in his formal evaluation narrative:

> At the middle school level, it is beneficial when students can see a common strand run through their instructional day. When something learned in science is tied to something learned in English, both make more sense. When instruction is coordinated from subject to subject and then from one grade level to the next, we not only have good education, we have magic. And that is what Lynne, Lourdes, and Sara created. . . . Participating in the reflective discussion related to the alternative evaluation project was an evaluation-supervision highlight for me. We spoke about the writing process, genres, cross-grade and cross-subject education, staff development opportunities, standards, the need to share learning experiences, validation, and a host of other things.[4]

It is possible for evaluation to be structured in ways that support this collective perspective. However, it is equally possible for individually focused and competitively oriented evaluation and compensation practices to undermine collegial work, harming the chances for professional sharing and learning. If teachers are ranked against one another, and if rewards are allocated on a competitive basis, evaluation is likely to undermine efforts toward collective improvements, to the ultimate detriment of teacher and student learning.

Collegiality is encouraged when teachers' contributions to school improvement and collaboration with peers and parents are valued

> **When instruction is coordinated from subject to subject and then from one grade level to the next, we not only have good education, we have magic.**

among the evaluation criteria, and when opportunities for analyzing teaching and learning are taken up by teaching teams and interwoven with opportunities for peer coaching and planning. As I discussed in Chapters 6 and 7, productive professional learning and effective coaching require communal engagement in sustained work on instruction over time. Successful practices also engage teams of teachers and administrators in the design and governance of the evaluation system, so that everyone develops shared standards of practice and a collective perspective on how to improve the work.

CONCLUSION

Comprehensive, coherent systems of teacher development and evaluation are needed to meet our goals of a quality education for all students. The key features of such systems (summarized in the box: Criteria for an Effective Teacher Evaluation System) can be seen in many schools and districts, although few places have stitched together all the components in a single tapestry. That is the critical work ahead.

Models offered throughout this book from around the United States and around the world can provide entry points for districts,

> **Models offered throughout this book from around the United States and around the world can provide entry points for districts, states, teachers, and unions to begin building systems that link evaluation, professional development, and collegial learning to support a teaching force that grows in expertise, retains its best teachers, and improves or removes those who cannot teach effectively.**

states, teachers, and unions to begin building systems that link evaluation, professional development, and collegial learning to support a teaching force that grows in expertise, retains its best teachers, and improves or removes those who cannot teach effectively. All of these goals are critical if, at the end of the day, teachers are to have the capacity to meet the diverse needs of the students they are committed to serve.

CRITERIA FOR AN EFFECTIVE TEACHER EVALUATION SYSTEM

1. **Teacher evaluation should be based on professional teaching standards** and should be sophisticated enough to assess teaching quality across the continuum of development, from novice to expert teacher.
2. **Evaluations should include multifaceted evidence of teacher practice, student learning, and professional contributions** that are considered in an integrated fashion, in relation to one another and to the teaching context. Any assessments used to make judgments about students' progress should be appropriate for the specific curriculum and students the teacher teaches.
3. **Evaluators should be knowledgeable about instruction and well trained in the evaluation system**, including the process of how to give productive feedback and how to support ongoing learning for teachers. As often as possible, and always at critical decision-making junctures (e.g., tenure or renewal), the evaluation team should include experts in the specific teaching field.
4. **Evaluation should be accompanied by useful feedback, and connected to professional development opportunities** that are relevant to teachers' goals and needs, including both formal learning opportunities and peer collaboration, observation, and coaching.
5. **The evaluation system should value and encourage teacher collaboration,** both in the standards and criteria that are used to assess teachers' work and in the way results are used to shape professional learning opportunities.
6. **Expert teachers should be part of the assistance and review process** for new teachers and for teachers needing extra assistance. They can provide the additional subject-specific expertise and person-power needed to ensure that intensive and effective assistance is offered and that decisions about tenure and continuation are well grounded.
7. **Panels of teachers and administrators should oversee the evaluation process** to ensure that it is thorough and of high quality, as well as fair and reliable. Such panels have been shown to facilitate more timely and well-grounded personnel decisions that avoid grievances and litigation. Teachers and school leaders should be involved in developing, implementing, and monitoring the system to ensure that it reflects good teaching well, that it operates effectively, that it is tied to useful learning opportunities for teachers, and that it produces valid results.

Student Learning Evidence Template: Albuquerque, New Mexico

STUDENT X

I. Introduction

Age:

Grade Level:

Subject or Discipline Area:

Number of Students in Class:

Names of Concepts, Understandings, or Skills Illustrated:

How the Student's Level of Work Compares to Others in His/Her Class:

II. Explanation of Student X's Learning

A. Why you selected this student (details about the student and his/her learning)

B. What the pieces of work represent

C. What you can say about where the student started

D. The steps that were taken to support the student's learning (including the student's own understanding of his/her learning)

E. How the student's progress was communicated to him/her and his/her parents

III. Examples of Student X Work over Time (3 to 5 examples, each dated and briefly explained). What evidence do the samples show of student progress and learning in relation to the concepts and skills identified earlier?

IV. Resources Used to Support Student Learning (Artifacts and descriptions of what resources/activities/teaching strategies you used to support student learning.)

V. Next Steps for This Student (Your analysis of what will next support the student's learning most effectively.)

STUDENT Y

I. Introduction

Age:

Grade Level:

Subject or Discipline Area:

Number of Students in Class:

Names of Concepts, Understandings, or Skills Illustrated:

How the Student's Level of Work Compares to Others in His/Her Class:

II. Explanation of Student Y's Learning

    A. Why you selected this student (details about the student and his/her learning)

    B. What the pieces of work represent

    C. What you can say about where the student started

    D. The steps that were taken to support the student's learning (including the student's own understanding of his/her learning)

    E. How the student's progress was communicated to him/her and his/her parents

III. Examples of Student Y's Work over Time (3 to 5 examples, each dated and briefly explained). What evidence do the samples show of student progress and learning in relation to the concepts and skills identified earlier?

IV. Resources Used to Support Student Learning (Artifacts and descriptions of what resources/activities/teaching strategies you used to support student learning.)

V. Next Steps for This Student (Your analysis of what will next support the student's learning most effectively.)

Conclusion

VI. What you have learned about your practice from analyzing student learning

Notes

Chapter 1

[1] Accomplished California Teachers (2010), p. 2.
[2] Wise, Darling-Hammond, McLaughlin, & Bernstein (1984).
[3] Accomplished California Teachers (2010), pp. 6–7.
[4] Duffet, Farkas, Rothertham, & Silva (2008).
[5] Accomplished California Teachers (2010), p. xx.
[6] Accomplished California Teachers (2010), p. 14.
[7] Hanushek (2011).
[8] For discussions of Finland's approach to teaching, see Darling-Hammond (2010) and Sahlberg (2012).
[9] Buchberger & Buchberger (2004), p. 10.
[10] Buchberger & Buchberger (2004), p. 6.
[11] From Darling-Hammond (2010). See also Sahlberg (2012).
[12] For a summary of studies, see Darling-Hammond & Bransford (2005); Darling-Hammond (2000); Wilson, Floden, & Ferrini-Mundy (2001).
[13] *Williams v. California*; Oakes (2004).
[14] Darling-Hammond (2002).
[15] Oakes (2004).
[16] National Association of State Boards of Education (NASBE) Study Group on Teacher Preparation, Retention, Evaluation, and Compensation (2011).

Chapter 2

[1] Yuan & Le (2012).
[2] The RAND study used level 4 from Webb's Depth of Knowledge taxonomy as the framework for its analysis of deeper learning skills. For a description of this taxonomy, see Webb, Alt, Ely, & Vesperman (2005).
[3] Herman and Linn (2013).
[4] Drawn from Wei, Darling-Hammond, Andree, Richardson, & Orphanos (2009), p. 21; see also Fernandez (2002).
[5] Baratz-Snowden (1990), p. 19.
[6] Accomplished California Teachers (2010), p. 12.
[7] National Board for Professional Teaching Standards (NBPTS) (2001).
[8] Haynes (1995), p. 60.
[9] Quoted in Toch & Rothman (2008).

Chapter 3

[1] Darling-Hammond & Wei (2009); Pecheone & Chung (2006).
[2] Ayers (1988); Dybdahl, Shaw, & Edwards (1997); Haney, Madaus, & Kreitzer (1987); Wilson, Hallam, Pecheone, & Moss (2012).

[3] See, for example, Bond, Smith, Baker, & Hattie (2000); Cavaluzzo (2004); Goldhaber & Anthony (2005); Smith, Gordon, Colby, & Wang (2005); Vandevoort, Amrein-Beardsley, & Berliner (2004).

[4] Wilson & Hallum (2006).

[5] Newton (2010); Darling-Hammond, Newton, & Wei (2012).

[6] National Education Association (2012).

[7] American Federation of Teachers (2012).

[8] For more information, see http://tpafieldtest.nesinc.com/

[9] Amee Adkins, Voices from the Field. Retrieved from: http://edtpa.aacte.org/voices-from-the-field

[10] Hanby (2011).

[11] Marcy Singer Gabella, Voices from the Field. Retrieved from: http://edtpa.aacte.org/voices-from-the-field

[12] Renner (2012).

[13] Pecheone & Stansbury (1996).

[14] Athanases (1994).

[15] Sato, Wei, & Darling-Hammond (2008); Tracz, Sienty, & Mata (1994); Tracz et al. (1995).

[16] This process is documented in the film *The Mitchell 20,* Randy Murray Productions. http://www.mitchell20.com/

[17] Berry (2009).

[18] Dean (forthcoming).

[19] See http://teachnm.org/experienced-teachers/professional-development-dossier.html

[20] New Mexico Public Education Department (2005).

[21] This account is drawn from Radoslovich & Roberts (2013).

Chapter 4

[1] Accomplished California Teachers (2010), p. 19.

[2] Skinner (2010).

[3] Milanowski, Kimball, & White (2004).

[4] The San Mateo Union High School District teacher evaluation handbook can be found at http://smuhsd.ca.schoolloop.com/file/1224132524944/1257605326962/7291446584551382814.pdf

[5] Milanowski et al. (2004).

[6] Jackson & Bruegmann (2009).

[7] Goddard & Goddard (2007).

[8] MetLife Foundation (2009).

[9] Darling-Hammond & Rothman (2011).

[10] Odden, Kelley, Heneman, & Milanowski (2001).

[11] Odden et al. (2001).

[12] Black & Wiliam (1998).

[13] See Darling-Hammond & Bransford (2005) for example.

[14] Valdés, Bunch, Snow, Lee, & Matos (2006).

[15] Rochester City School District (2012).

[16] Packard & Dereshiwsky (1991).

Chapter 5

[1] Amrein-Beardsley (2012).

[2] This account is drawn from an analysis by Aaron Pallas (2012).

[3] Pallas (2012).

[4] See for example, Sentell (2012); Watanabe (2012).

[5] National Research Council (2010).
[6] Harris (2012), p. 4.
[7] Harris & Anderson (2011). See also Jackson (2012); Newton, Darling-Hammond, Haertel, & Thomas (2010).
[8] Koedel & Betts (2009).
[9] Amrein-Beardsley & Collins (2012); Sentell (2012).
[10] Sentell (2012).
[11] Harris (2012).
[12] For reviews, see Braun (2005); McCaffrey, Lockwood, Koretz, & Hamilton (2005).
[13] Braun (2005), p. 10.
[14] Rivkin, Hanushek, & Kain (2000).
[15] See, for example, Goldhaber, Brewer, & Anderson (1999).
[16] Alexander, Entwisle, & Olson (2007).
[17] Rubin, Stuart, & Zanutto (2004), p. 113.
[18] Braun (2005), p. 17.
[19] McCaffrey, Koretz, Lockwood, & Hamilton (2005).
[20] Sass (2008); see also Newton, Darling-Hammond, Haertel, & Thomas (2010) for similar findings.
[21] Chart from J. Rothstein, based on data from Sass (2008).
[22] National Research Council, Board on Testing and Assessment (2009).
[23] Newton et al. (2010).
[24] Harris & Anderson (2011); Jackson (2012); Newton et al. (2010).
[25] Amrein-Beardsley & Collins (2012).
[26] Amrein-Beardsley & Collins (2012), p. 16.
[27] Amrein-Beardsley & Collins (2012), p. 16.
[28] Briggs & Domingue (2011); Rothstein (2010).
[29] Lockwood et al. (2007).
[30] Bill & Melinda Gates Foundation (2010); Rothstein (2011).
[31] Lockwood et al. (2007).
[32] Corcoran, Jennings, & Beveridge (2011).
[33] Education Week (2001); Hoffman, Assaf, & Paris (2001); Jones & Egley (2004).
[34] Southeast Center for Teaching Quality (2003), p. 15.
[35] (Haney, 2000, part 6, p. 10).
[36] For a summary of these concerns, see Baker et al. (2010).
[37] Baker et al. (2010), p. 8.
[38] See http://www.newyorkprincipals.org/appr-paper
[39] Fryer (2011); Springer et al. (2010).
[40] Martins (2009).
[41] Mathews (2008).
[42] For more detail about the Denver Procomp system, see http://denverprocomp.org
[43] Long Beach Unified School District (2003).
[44] Berry & Daughtrey, with Moore, Orphal, & Ratzel (2012).
[45] Lachlan-Haché, Cushing, & Bivona (2012a), p. 6.
[46] Lachlan-Haché, Cushing, & Bivona (2012b), p. 2.
[47] Rhode Island Department of Education (RIDE) (2013).
[48] See http://www.ride.ri.gov/EducatorQuality/EducatorEvaluation/SLO.aspx

Chapter 6

[1] Wei, Darling-Hammond, Andree, Richardson, & Orphanos (2009).
[2] Accomplished California Teachers (2010), p. 7.

[3] Wei, Darling-Hammond, Andree, Richardson, & Orphanos (2009).

[4] Yoon, Duncan, Lee, Scarloss, & Shapley (2007).

[5] Darling-Hammond & Richardson (2009).

[6] Darling-Hammond et al. (2009).

[7] Darling-Hammond et al. (2009).

[8] Wei, Darling-Hammond, & Adamson (2010).

[9] This section draws on Darling-Hammond et al. (2009).

[10] Cohen & Hill (2001); Desimone, Porter, Garet, Yoon, & Birman. (2002); Garet, Porter, Desimone, Birman, & Yoon (2001); Supovitz, Mayer, & Kahle (2000); Weiss & Pasley (2006).

[11] Corcoran, McVay, & Riordan (2003); Supovitz & Turner (2000); Banilower (2002).

[12] Garet et al. (2001).

[13] Wei et al. (2010).

[14] Cohen & Hill (2001); Garet et al. (2001); Desimone et al. (2002); Penuel, Fishman, Yamaguchi, & Gallagher (2007); Saxe, Gearhart, & Nasir (2001); Supovitz, et al., (2000).

[15] Garet et al. (2001).

[16] Blank, de las Alas, & Smith (2007); Cohen & Hill (2001); Lieberman & Wood (2002); Merek & Methven (1991); Saxe et al. (2001).

[17] Merek & Methven (1991).

[18] Ball & Cohen (1999); Dunne, Nave, & Lewis (2000); Little (2003).

[19] Strahan (2003).

[20] Cohen & Hill (2001); Garet et al. (2001); Penuel et al. (2007); Supovitz et al. (2000).

[21] Supovitz et al. (2000).

[22] Hord (1997); Joyce & Calhoun (1996); Louis, Marks, & Kruse (1996); McLaughlin & Talbert (2001); Newman & Wehlage (1997).

[23] Dunne et al. (2000).

[24] Bryk, Camburn, & Louis (1999); Calkins, Guenther, Belfiore, & Lash (2007); Goddard, Goddard, & Tschannen-Moran (2007); Louis & Marks (1998); Supovitz & Christman (2003).

[25] Newman & Wehlage (1997).

[26] Mindich & Lieberman (2012).

[27] Professional Development Partnership (2008).

[28] Elmore (1996).

[29] Solomon, White, Cohen & Woo (2007).

[30] Agam, Reifsneider, & Diana Wardell (2006).

[31] The TAP teacher responsibility rubrics were designed based on several teacher accountability systems currently in use, including the Rochester (New York) Career in Teaching Program, Douglas County (Colorado) *Teacher's Performance Pay Plan*, Vaughn Next Century Charter School (Los Angeles, CA) Performance Pay Plan, and Rolla (Missouri) School District Professional Based Teacher Evaluation.

[32] Culbertson (2012), p. 16.

[33] Solomon, White, Cohen, & Woo (2007).

[34] Darling-Hammond (2010).

[35] Organisation for Economic Co-operation and Development (2007).

[36] Organisation for Economic Co-operation and Development (2007).

[37] Wei et al. (2010).

[38] Darling-Hammond (1999); Miles & Darling-Hammond (1998).

[39] Miles & Darling-Hammond (1998).

[40] Sarason (1982).

[41] Darling-Hammond et al. (2009).

[42] The Nation's Report Card. Retrieved from http://nces.ed.gov/nationsreportcard/states/
[43] Darling-Hammond (2010).
[44] Tan (2012).
[45] Tan (2012).
[46] Tripp (2004).
[47] Hargreaves (2008).

Chapter 7

[1] Darling-Hammond, Meyerson, LaPointe, & Orr (2009).
[2] Daley & Kim (2010).
[3] TAP website, http://www.tapsystem.org/action/action.taf?page=saying
[4] Darling-Hammond, Meyerson et al. (2009), p. xxx.
[5] California State University Institute for Education Reform (2000); Humphrey, Koppich, Bland, & Bosetti (2011); National Commission on Teaching and America's Future (1996).
[6] Humphrey et al. (2011).
[7] Harvard Graduate School of Education (n.d.).
[8] Humphrey et al. (2011).
[9] Marshall (2008).
[10] Harvard Graduate School of Education (n.d.).
[11] Humphrey et al. (2011).
[12] California State University Institute for Education Reform (2000).
[13] Accomplished California Teachers (2010).
[14] Humphrey et al. (2011), p. 31.
[15] Center for Teaching Quality, as cited in ACT (2012), p. 31.
[16] Winerip (2011).
[17] Winerip (2011).
[18] Anderson (2012).
[19] Strunk, Weinstein, Makkonen, & Furedi (2012), p. 49.
[20] Strunk et al. (2012), p. 49.
[21] Wise & Darling-Hammond (1984/1985).
[22] Anderson (2012).
[23] Anderson (2012).
[24] Turque (2009); Strauss (2010).
[25] Accomplished California Teachers (2010), p. 2.

Chapter 8

[1] Toch & Rothman (2008), p. 13.
[2] Supovitz (2012).
[3] Accomplished California Teachers (2012), p. 20.
[4] Accomplished California Teachers (2012), p. 20.

References

Accomplished California Teachers (ACT). (2010). *A quality teacher in every classroom: Creating a teacher evaluation system that works for California.* Stanford, CA: National Board Resource Center, Stanford University.

Agam, K., Reifsneider, D., & Wardell, D. (2006). The Teacher Advancement Program: National Teacher Attitudes. Available at http://www.tapsystem.org/publications/publications.taf?page=reports_archived

Alexander, K. L., Entwisle, D. R., & Olson, L. S. (2007). Lasting consequences of the summer learning gap. *American Sociological Review, 72,* 167–180.

American Federation of Teachers. (2012). *Raising the bar: Aligning and elevating teacher preparation and the teaching profession.* Washington, DC: Author.

Amrein-Beardsley, A., & Collins, C. (2012). *The SAS® (EVAAS®) Education Value-Added Assessment System: Intended and unintended consequences. Education Policy Analysis Archives,* 20(12). Available at http://epaa.asu.edu/ojs/article/view/1096

Anderson, J. (2012, February 19). States try to fix quirks in teacher evaluations. *New York Times.* Available at http://www.nytimes.com/2012/02/20/education/states-address-problems-with-teacher-evaluations.html?_r=1&pagewanted=print

Athanases, S. (1994). Teachers' reports of the effects of preparing portfolios of literacy instruction. *Elementary School Journal,* 94(4), 421–439.

Ayers, J. B. (1988). Another look at the concurrent and predictive validity of the National Teacher Examinations. *Journal of Educational Research, 81,* 133–137.

Baker, E. L., Barton, P. E., Darling-Hammond, L., Haertel, E., Ladd, H. F., Linn, R. L., Ravitch, D. Rothstein, R. Shavelson, R. J., & Shepard L. A. (2010). *Problems with the use of test scores to evaluate teachers.* Washington, DC: Economic Policy Institute.

Ball, D., & Cohen, D. (1999). Developing practice, developing practitioners: Toward a practice-based theory of professional education. In L. Darling-Hammond & G. Sykes (Eds.), *Teaching as the learning profession: Handbook of policy and practice* (pp. 3–32). San Francisco, CA: Jossey-Bass.

Banilower, E. R. (2002). *Results of the 2001–2002 study of the impact of the local systemic change initiative on student achievement in science.* Chapel Hill, NC: Horizon Research.

Baratz-Snowden, J. (1990). The NBPTS begins its research and development program. *Educational Researcher,* 19(6), 19–24.

Berry, B. (2009). *Keeping the promise: Recruiting, retaining, and growing effective teachers for high-needs schools.* Raleigh, NC: Center for Teaching Quality.

Berry, B., & Daughtrey, A., with Moore, R., Orphal, D., & Ratzel, M. (2012). *New student assessments and advancing teaching as a results-oriented profession.* Washington, DC: Arabella Advisers.

Bill & Melinda Gates Foundation. (2010). *Learning about teaching: Initial findings from the Measures of Effective Teaching Project.* Seattle: Author.

Black, P., & Wiliam, D. (1998). Assessment and classroom learning. *Assessment and Education: Principles, Policy And Practice, 5*(1), 7–75.

Blank, R. K., de las Alas, N., & Smith, C. (2007). *Analysis of the quality of professional development programs for mathematics and science teachers: Findings from a cross-state study.* Washington DC: Council of Chief State School Officers.

Bond, L., Smith, T., Baker, W., & Hattie, J. (2000). *The certification system of the National Board for Professional Teaching Standards: A construct and consequential validity study.* Greensboro, NC: Center for Educational Research and Evaluation.

Braun, H. (2005). *Using student progress to evaluate teachers: A primer on value-added models.* Princeton, NJ: ETS Policy Information Center.

Briggs, D., & Domingue, B. (2011). *Due diligence and the evaluation of teachers: A review of the value-added analysis underlying the effectiveness rankings of Los Angeles Unified School District teachers by the* Los Angeles Times. Boulder, CO: National Education Policy Center.

Bryk, A., Camburn, E., & Louis, K. (1999). Professional community in Chicago elementary schools: Facilitating factors and organizational consequences. *Educational Administration Quarterly, 35*(5), 751–781.

Buchberger, F., & Buchberger, I. (2004). Problem-solving capacity of a teacher education system as a condition of success? An analysis of the "Finnish Case," In F. Buchberger & S. Berghammer (Eds.), *Education policy analysis in a comparative perspective* (pp. 222–237). Linz: Trauner.

California State University Institute for Education Reform. (2000, March). *Peer assistance and review: Working models across the country.* Sacramento: Author.

Calkins, A., Guenther, W., Belfiore, G., & Lash, D. (2007). *The turnaround challenge: Why America's best opportunity to dramatically improve student achievement lies in our worst-performing schools.* Boston: Mass Insight Education & Research Institute.

Cavaluzzo, L. (2004). *Is National Board Certification an effective signal of teacher quality?* (National Science Foundation No. REC-0107014). Alexandria, VA: The CNA Corporation.

Cohen, D. K., & Hill, H. C. (2000). Instructional policy and classroom performance: The mathematics reform in California. *Teachers College Record, 102,* 294–343.

Corcoran, S. P., Jennings, J. L., & Beveridge, A. A. (2011). Teacher effectiveness on high- and low-stakes tests. Working paper, New York University.

Corcoran, T., McVay, S., & Riordan, K. (2003). *Getting it right: The MISE approach to professional development.* Philadelphia: Consortium for Policy Research in Education.

Culbertson, J. (2012, November). Putting the value in teacher evaluation. *Phi Delta Kappan, 94*(3), 14–18.

Daley, G., & Kim, L. (2010). *A teacher evaluation system that works.* Santa Monica, CA: National Institute for Excellence in Teaching.

Darling-Hammond, L. (1999, Spring). Target time toward teachers. *Journal of Staff Development, 20*(2), 31–36.

Darling-Hammond, L. (2000). Teacher quality and student achievement: A review of state policy evidence. *Educational Policy Analysis Archives, 8*(1). Available at http://epaa.asu.edu/epaa/v8n1

Darling-Hammond, L. (2002). *Access to quality teaching: An analysis of inequality in California's public schools.* Los Angeles: UCLA, Institute for Democracy, Education, & Access. Williams Watch Series: Investigating the Claims of *Williams v. State of California.* Paper wws-rr002-1002. Available at http://repositories.cdlib.org/idea/wws/wws-rr002-1002

Darling-Hammond, L. (2010). *The flat world and education: How America's commitment to equity will determine our future.* New York: Teachers College Press.

Darling-Hammond, L., & Bransford, J. (2005). *Preparing teachers for a changing world: What teachers should learn and be able to do.* San Francisco: Jossey-Bass.

Darling-Hammond, L., Meyerson, D., LaPointe, M., & Orr, M. (2009). *Preparing principals for a changing world.* San Francisco: Jossey-Bass.

Darling-Hammond, L., Newton, S. P., & Wei, R. C. (2012). *Developing and assessing beginning teacher effectiveness: The potential of performance assessments.* Stanford, CA: Stanford Center for Opportunity Policy in Education. Available at http://edpolicy.stanford.edu/sites/default/files/publications/developing-and-assessing-beginning-teacher-effectiveness-potential-performance-assessments.pdf

Darling-Hammond, L., & Richardson, N. (2009, February). Teacher learning: What matters? *Educational Leadership, 5*(66), 46–53.

Darling-Hammond, L., & Rothman, R. (2011). *Teacher and leader effectiveness in high-performing education systems.* Washington, DC: Alliance for Excellent Education and Stanford, CA: Stanford Center for Opportunity Policy in Education.

Darling-Hammond, L., & Wei, R. C. (2009). Teacher preparation and teacher learning: A changing policy landscape. In G. Sykes (Ed.), *The handbook of education policy research* (pp. 613–636). Washington DC: American Education Research Association.

Dean, S. (in press). *Developing effective communities of practice through National Board Certification.* Stanford, CA: National Board Resource Center and the Stanford Center for Opportunity Policy in Education.

Desimone, L. M., Porter, A. C., Garet, M. S., Yoon, K. S., & Birman, B. F. (2002). Effects of professional development on teachers' instruction: Results from a three-year longitudinal study. *Educational Evaluation and Policy Analysis, 24,* 81–112.

Duffett, A., Farkas, S., Rothertham, A. J., & Silva, E. (2008). *Waiting to be won over: Teachers speak on the profession, unions, and reform.* Washington, DC: Education Sector.

Dunne, F., Nave, B., & Lewis, A. (2000). Critical friends: Teachers helping to improve student learning. *Phi Delta Kappa International Research Bulletin (CEDR), 28,* 9–12. Available at http://www.pdkintl.org/edres/resbul28.htm

Dybdahl, C. S., Shaw, D. G., & Edwards, D. (1997). Teacher testing: Reason or rhetoric. *Journal of Research and Development in Education, 30*(4), 248–254.

Education Week. (2001). *Quality counts 2001: A better balance.* Bethesda, MD: Editorial Projects in Education.

Elmore, R. (1996). Getting to scale with good educational practice. *Harvard Educational Review, 66*(1), 1–26.

Fernandez, C. (2002). Learning from Japanese approaches to professional development: The case of lesson study. *Journal of Teacher Education, 53*(5), 393–405.

Fryer, R. G. (2011). *Teacher incentives and student achievement: Evidence from New York City public schools* (NBER Working Paper no. 16850). Cambridge, MA: National Bureau of Economic Research.

Garet, M., Porter, A., Desimone, L., Birman, B., & Yoon, K. S. (2001). What makes professional development effective? Results from a national sample of teachers. *American Educational Research Journal, 38*(4), 915–945.

Goddard, Y. L., Goddard, R. D., & Tschannen-Moran, M. (2007). Theoretical and empirical investigation of teacher collaboration for school improvement and student achievement tin public elementary schools. *Teachers College Record, 109*(4), 877–896.

Goldhaber, D., & Anthony, E. (2005). *Can teacher quality be effectively assessed?* Seattle: University of Washington and the Urban Institute.

Goldhaber, D., Brewer, D., & Anderson, D. (1999). A three-way error components analysis of educational productivity. *Education Economics, 7*(3), 199–208.

Hanby, D. (2011, October). *Pioneer reflections from Ohio's 2010–11 journey: Pilot year insights from Leg I and Leg II travelers.* Presentation at the Ohio Council of Teacher Educators Conference, Columbus, Ohio.

Haney, W. (2000). The myth of the Texas miracle in education. *Educational Policy Analysis Archives,* (41): http://epaa.asu.edu/epaa/v8n41/

Haney, W., Madaus, G., & Kreitzer, A. (1987). Charms talismanic: Testing teachers for the improvement of American education. In E. Z. Rothkopf (Ed.), *Review of research in education* (Vol. 14, pp. 169–238). Washington, DC: American Educational Research Association.

Hanushek, E. (2011). Lifting student achievement by weeding out harmful teachers. Available at http://www.eduwonk.com/2011/10/lifting-student-achievement-by-weeding-out-harmful-teachers.html

Hargreaves, A. (2008). The coming of post-standardization: Three weddings and a funeral. In C. Sugrue (Ed.), *The future of educational change: International perspectives* (pp. 15–33). New York: Routledge.

Harris, D. (2012, October). How do value-added indicators compare to other measures of teacher effectiveness? Available at http://carnegieknowledgenetwork.org/briefs/value-added/value-added-other-measures/

Harris, D., & Anderson, A. (2011, March). Bias of public sector worker performance monitoring: Theory and empirical evidence from middle school teachers. Paper presented at the annual meeting of the Association for Education Finance and Policy, Seattle, WA.

Harris, D., Sass, T. R., & Semykina, A. (2010). Value-added models and the measurement of teacher productivity. Available at http://www.caldercenter.org/UploadedPDF/1001508-Measurement-of-Teacher-Productivity.pdf

Harvard Graduate School of Education. (n.d.). A user's guide to peer assistance and review. Available at http://www.gse.harvard.edu/~ngt/par/

Haynes, D. D. (1995). One teacher's experience with National Board assessment. *Educational Leadership, 52*(8), 58–60.

Herman, J. L., & Linn, R. L. (2013). *On the road to assessing deeper learning: The status of Smarter Balanced and PARCC assessment consortia* (CRESST Report 823). Los Angeles: University of California, National Center for Research on Evaluation, Standards, and Student Testing (CRESST).

Hoffman, J. V., Assaf, L. C., & Paris, S. G. (2001). High stakes testing in reading: Today in Texas, tomorrow? *The Reading Teacher, 54*(5), 482–492.

Hord, S. (1997). *Professional learning communities: Communities of continuous inquiry and improvement.* Austin, TX: Southwest Educational Development Laboratory.

Humphrey, D., Koppich, J., Bland, A., & Bosetti, K. R. (2011). *Peer review: Getting serious about teacher evaluation.* Menlo Park, CA: SRI International and J. Koppich & Associates.

Jackson, C. K. (2012). *Teacher quality at the high school level: The importance of accounting for tracks.* Washington, DC: National Bureau of Economic Research.

Jackson, C. K., & Bruegmann, E. (2009, August). *Teaching students and teaching each other: The importance of peer learning for teachers.* Washington, DC: National Bureau of Economic Research.

Jones, B. D., & Egley R. J. (2004). Voices from the frontlines: Teachers' perceptions of high-stakes testing. *Education Policy Analysis Archives, 12*(39). Available at http://epaa.asu.edu/epaa/v12n39/

Joyce, B., & Calhoun, E. (1996). *Learning experiences in school renewal: An exploration of five successful programs.* Eugene, OR: ERIC Clearinghouse on Educational Management.

Koedel, C., & Betts, J. (2009). *Value-added to what? How a ceiling in the testing instrument influences value-added estimation* (NBER Working Paper 14778, National Bureau of Economic Research). Available at http://www.nber.org/papers/w14778

Lachlan-Haché, L., Cushing, E., & Bivona, L. (2012a). *Student learning objectives as measures of educator effectiveness: The basics.* Washington, DC: American Institutes of Research.

Lachlan-Haché, L., Cushing, E., & Bivona, L. (2012b). *Student learning objectives: Benefits, challenges, and solutions.* Washington, DC: American Institutes of Research.

Lieberman, A., & Wood, D. (2002). From network learning to classroom teaching. *Journal of Educational Change, 3,* 315–337.

Little, J. W. (2003). Inside teacher community: Representations of classroom practice. *Teacher College Record, 105*(6), 913–945.

Lockwood, J. R., McCaffrey, D. F., Hamilton, L. S., Stetcher, B., Lee, V. N., & Martinez, J. F. (2007). The sensitivity of value-added teacher effect estimates to different mathematics achievement measures. *Journal of Educational Measurement, 44*(1), 47–67.

Long Beach Unified School District. (2003). *Teacher evaluation handbook.* Long Beach, CA: Author.

Louis, K. S., & Marks, H. M. (1998). Does professional learning community affect the classroom? Teachers' work and student experiences in restructuring schools. *American Journal of Education, 106*(4), 532–575.

Louis, K. S., Marks, H. M., & Kruse, S. (1996). Professional community in restructuring schools. *American Educational Research Journal, 33*(4), 757–798.

Marshall, R. (2008). *The case for collaborative school reform: The Toledo experience.* Washington, DC: Economic Policy Institute.

Martins, P. (2009). *Individual teacher incentives, student achievement and grade inflation* (Discussion Paper No. 4051). London: Queen Mary, University of London, CEG-IST and IZA.

Mathews, J. (2008, October 6). Merit pay could ruin teamwork. *Washington Post,* p. B02.

McCaffrey, D. F., Koretz, D., Lockwood, J. R., & Hamilton, L. S. (2005). *Evaluating value-added models for teacher accountability.* Santa Monica, CA: RAND Corporation.

McLaughlin, M. W., & Talbert, J. E. (2001). *Professional communities and the work of high school teaching.* Chicago: University of Chicago Press.

Merek E., & Methven, S. (1991). Effects of the learning cycle upon student and classroom teacher performance. *Journal of Research in Science Teaching, 28*(1), 41–53.

MetLife Foundation. (2009). *The MetLife survey of the American teacher: Collaborating for student success.* New York: Author.

Milanowski, A., Kimball, S. M., & White, B. (2004). *The relationship between standards-based teacher evaluation scores and student achievement.* Madison: University of Wisconsin-Madison, Consortium for Policy Research in Education.

Miles, K. H., & Darling-Hammond, L. (1998, Spring). Rethinking the allocation of teaching resources: Some lessons from high-performing schools. *Educational Evaluation and Policy Analysis, 20.*

Mindich, D., & Lieberman, A. (2012). *Building a learning community: A tale of two schools.* Stanford, CA: Stanford Center for Opportunity Policy and Education.

National Association of State Boards of Education (NASBE) Study Group on Teacher Preparation, Retention, Evaluation, and Compensation. (2011). *Gearing up: Creating a systemic approach to teacher effectiveness.* Arlington, VA: Author.

National Board for Professional Teaching Standards (NBPTS). (2001). *The impact of National Board Certification on teachers: A survey of National Board certified teachers and assessors.* Arlington, VA: Author.

National Commission on Teaching and America's Future. (1996). *What matters most: Teaching for America's future.* New York: Author.

National Education Association. (2012). *Transforming teaching: Connecting professional responsibility with student learning.* Washington, DC: Author.

National Research Council. (2010). *Getting value out of value-added: Report of a workshop.* Washington, DC: Author.

National Research Council, Board on Testing and Assessment. (2009). *Letter report to the U.S. Department of Education.* Washington, DC: Author.

New Mexico Public Education Department. (2005). *New Mexico's 3-tiered licensure performance evaluation handbook.* Available at http://teachnm.org/uploads/docs/performance_eval_handbook.pdf

Newman, F., & Wehlage, G. (1997). *Successful school restructuring: A report to the public and educators by the Center on Organization and Restructuring of Schools.* Madison, WI: Document Service, Wisconsin Center for Education Research.

Newton, S. P. (2010). *Predictive validity of the performance assessment for California teachers.* Stanford, CA: Stanford Center for Opportunity Policy in Education. Available at http://scale.stanford.edu/

Newton, X., Darling-Hammond, L., Haertel, E., & Thomas, E. (2010). Value-added modeling of teacher effectiveness: An exploration of stability across models and contexts. *Educational Policy Analysis Archives, 18*(23). Available at http://epaa.asu.edu/ojs/article/view/810

Oakes, J. (2004). Investigating the claims in *Williams v. State of California*: An unconstitutional denial of education's basic tools? *Teachers College Record, 106*(10), 1889–1906.

Odden, A., Kelley, C., Heneman, H., & Milanowski, A. (2001, November). *Enhancing teacher quality through knowledge- and skills-based pay* (CPRE Policy Briefs, R-34). Philadelphia: Consortium for Policy Research in Education, University of Pennsylvania.

Organisation for Economic Co-operation and Development. (2007). Programme for International Student Assessment 2006: Science competencies for tomorrow's world. Paris: Author. Available at http://nces.ed.gov/surveys/pisa/index.asp

Packard, R., & Dereshiwsky, M. (1991). *Final quantitative assessment of the Arizona career ladder pilot-test project.* Flagstaff: Northern Arizona University.

Pallas, A. (2012, May 15). The worst eighth-grade math teacher in New York City. Available at http://eyeoned.org/content/the-worst-eighth-grade-math-teacher-in-new-york-city_326/

Pecheone, R. L., & Chung, R. R. (2006). Evidence in teacher education: The Performance Assessment for California Teachers (PACT). *Journal of Teacher Education, 57*(1), 22–36.

Pecheone, R. L., & Stansbury, K. (1996). Connecting teacher assessment and school reform. *Elementary School Journal, 97,* 163–177.

Penuel, W., Fishman, B., Yamaguchi, R., & Gallagher, L. (2007, December). What makes professional development effective? Strategies that foster curriculum implementation. *American Educational Research Journal, 44*(4), 921–958.

Professional Development Partnership. (2008). A common language for professional learning communities. Available at http://www.nj.gov/education/profdev/pd/teacher/common.pdf

Radoslovich, J., & Roberts, S. (2013). *Practitioner action research as a measure of teacher effectiveness.* South Valley Academy, New Mexico.

Rhode Island Department of Education (RIDE). (2013, January). Misconceptions & facts about student learning objectives. Available at http://www.ride.ri.gov/EducatorQuality/EducatorEvaluation/Docs/Misconceptions_and_Facts_about_SLOs.pdf

Rivkin, S. G., Hanushek, E. A., & Kain, J. F. (2000). *Teachers, schools, and academic achievement* [rev. ed.] (Working Paper No. 6691). Cambridge, MA: National Bureau of Economic Research.

Rochester City School District. (2012). Teacher evaluation guide, 2012–13. Available at http://www.nctq.org/docs/Rochester_Teacher_Evaluation_Guide_AUGUST_2012.pdf

Rothstein, J. (2010). Teacher quality in educational production: Tracking, decay, and student achievement. *Quarterly Journal of Economics, 125*(1), 175–214.

Rothstein, J. (2011). *Review of "Learning about teaching: Initial findings from the Measures of Effective Teaching Project."* Boulder, CO: National Education Policy Center.

Rubin, D. B., Stuart, E. A., & Zanutto, E. L. (2004). A potential outcomes view of value-added assessment in education. *Journal of Educational and Behavioral Statistics, 29*(1), 103–116.

Sahlberg, P. (2012). *Finnish lessons.* New York: Teachers College Press.

Sarason, S. B. (1982). *The culture of the school and the problem of change.* Boston: Allyn & Bacon. (Originally published 1971)

Sass, T. (2008). *The stability of value-added measures of teacher quality and implications for teacher compensation policy.* Washington DC: Calder.

Sato, M., Wei, R. C., & Darling-Hammond, L. (2008). Improving teachers' assessment practices through professional development: The case of National Board Certification. *American Educational Research Journal, 45,* 669–700.

Saxe, G., Gearhart, M., & Nasir, N. S. (2001). Enhancing students' understanding of Mathematics: A study of three contrasting approaches to professional support. *Journal of Mathematics Teacher Education, 4,* 55–79.

Sentell, W. (2012, October 16). Teachers: Educators at top schools fear new reviews will cost their jobs. *The Baton Rouge Advocate.* Available at http://theadvocate.com/home/4161514-125/teachers-reviews-threaten-their-jobs

Skinner, K. J. (2010). *Reinventing evaluation: Connecting professional practice with student learning.* Boston: Massachusetts Teachers Association.

Smith, T., Gordon, B., Colby, S., & Wang, J. (2005). *An examination of the relationship of the depth of student learning and National Board Certification status.* Boone, NC: Office for Research on Teaching, Appalachian State University.

Solomon, L., White, J. T., Cohen, D., & Woo, D. (2007). *The effectiveness of the Teacher Advancement Program.* Santa Monica, CA: National Institute for Excellence in Teaching.

Southeast Center for Teaching Quality. (2003, December 3–5). Teacher Leaders Network conversation: No Child Left Behind. Available at http://www.teacherleaders.org/old_site/Conversations/NCLB_chat_full.pdf

Springer, M. G., Ballou, D., Hamilton, L., Lee, V., Lockwood, J. R., McCaffrey, D. F., Pepper, M., & Stecher, B. M. (2010). *Teacher pay for performance: Experimental evidence from the Project on Incentives in Teaching.* Nashville, TN: National Center on Performance Incentives, Vanderbilt University.

Strahan, D. (2003). Promoting a collaborative professional culture in three elementary schools that have beaten the odds. *The Elementary School Journal, 104*(2), 127–133.

Strauss, V. (2010, July 23). The problem with how Rhee fired teachers. Available at http://voices.washingtonpost.com/answer-sheet/dc-schools/the-problem-with-how-rhee-fire.html

Strunk, K. O., Weinstein, T., Makkonen, R., & Furedi, D. (2012). Lessons learned. *Phi Delta Kappan, 94*(3), 47–51.

Supovitz, J. (2012). *The linking study—First year results: A report of the first year effects of an experimental study of the impact of feedback to teachers on teaching and learning.* Philadelphia: Graduate School of Education, University of Pennsylvania, Consortium for Policy Research in Education.

Supovitz, J. A., & Christman, J. B. (2003, November). *Developing communities of instructional practice: Lessons from Cincinnati and Philadelphia* (CPRE Policy Briefs RB-39). Philadelphia: University of Pennsylvania, Graduate School of Education.

Supovitz, J. A., Mayer, D. P. , & Kahle, J. B. (2000). Promoting inquiry based instructional practice: The longitudinal impact of professional development in the context of systemic reform. *Educational Policy, 14*(3), 331–356.

Supovitz, J. A., & Turner, H. M. (2000). The effects of professional development on science teaching practices and classroom culture. *Journal of Research in Science Teaching, 37*(9), 963–980.

Tan, O. (2012). Singapore's holistic approach to teacher development. *Phi Delta Kappan, 94*(3), 76–77.

Toch, T., & Rothman, R. (2008). *Rush to judgment: Teacher evaluation in public education.* Washington, DC: Education Sector.

Tracz, S. M., Sienty, S., & Mata, S. (1994, February). The self-reflection of teachers compiling portfolios for National Certification: Work in progress. Paper presented at the annual meeting of the American Association of Colleges for Teacher Education, Chicago.

Tracz, S. M., Sienty, S., Todorov, K., Snyder, J., Takashima, B., Pensabene, R., Olsen, B., Pauls, L., & Sork, J. (1995, April). Improvement in teaching skills: Perspectives from National Board for Professional Teaching Standards field test network candidates. Paper presented at the annual meeting of the American Educational Research Association, San Francisco.

Tripp, D. (2004). Teachers' networks: A new approach to the professional development of teachers in Singapore. In C. Day & J. Sachsm (Eds.), *International handbook on the continuing professional development of teachers* (pp. 191–214). Maidenhead, UK: Open University Press.

Turque, B. (2009, October 1). D.C. launches rigorous teacher evaluation system. Available at http://www.washingtonpost.com/wp-dyn/content/article/2009/09/30/AR2009093004729. html

Valdés, G., Bunch, G., Snow, C., Lee, C., & Matos, L. (2006). Enhancing the development of students' language(s). In L. Darling-Hammond & J. Bransford (Eds.), *Preparing teachers for a changing world: What teachers should learn and be able to do* (pp. 126–127). San Francisco: Jossey Bass.

Vandevoort, L. G., Amrein-Beardsley, A., & Berliner, D. C. (2004). National Board Certified teachers and their students' achievement. *Education Policy Analysis Archives, 12*(46), 117.

Watanabe, T. (2012, October 28). Measuring the worth of a teacher? L.A. Unified School District's Academic Growth Over Time measurement system, based on students' progress on standardized tests, spurs debate over fairness, accuracy. Available at http://articles.latimes.com/2012/oct/28/local/la-me-teacher-evals-20121029

Webb, N. L., Alt, M., Ely, R., & Vesperman, B. (2005). Web alignment tool (WAT): Training manual 1.1. Available at http://www.wcer.wisc.edu/WAT/Training%20Manual%202.1%20Draft%20091205.doc

Wei, R. C., Darling-Hammond, L., & Adamson, F. (2010). *Professional learning in the United States: Trends and challenges.* Dallas, TX: National Staff Development Council and Stanford, CA: Stanford Center for Opportunity Policy and Education.

Wei, R. C., Darling-Hammond, L., Andree, A., Richardson, N., & Orphanos, S. (2009). *Professional learning in the learning profession: A status report on teacher development in the United States and abroad.* Dallas, TX: National Staff Development Council and Stanford, CA: Stanford Center for Opportunity Policy and Education.

Weiss, I. R., & Pasley, J. D. (2006). *Scaling up instructional improvement through teacher professional development: Insights from the local systemic change initiative.* Philadelphia: Consortium for Policy Research in Education (CPRE) Policy Briefs.

Wilson, M., & Hallum, P. J. (2006). *Using student achievement test scores as evidence of external validity for indicators of teacher quality: Connecticut's Beginning Educator Support and Training program.* Berkeley: University of California at Berkeley.

Wilson, M., Hallum, P. J., Pecheone, R., & Moss, P. (2012). Using student achievement test scores as evidence of external validity for indicators of teacher quality: Connecticut's Beginning Educator Support and Training Program. Berkeley, CA: Berkeley Educational Assessment and Research Center.

Wilson, S. M., Floden, R., & Ferrini-Mundy, J. (2001). *Teacher preparation research: Current knowledge, gaps, and recommendations.* Seattle: Center for the Study of Teaching and Policy, University of Washington.

Winerip, M. (2011, November 6). In Tennessee, following the rules for evaluations off a cliff. Available at http://www.nytimes.com/2011/11/07/education/tennessees-rules-on-teacher-evaluations-bring-frustration.html?_r=2&scp=1&sq=michael%20winerip%20tennessee&st=cse

Wise, A. E., & Darling-Hammond, L. (1984/1985). Teacher evaluation and teacher professionalism. *Educational Leadership, 42*(4), 28–33.

Wise, A. E., Darling-Hammond, L., McLaughlin, M. W., & Bernstein, H. T. (1984). *Teacher evaluation: A study of effective practices.* Santa Monica, CA: RAND Corporation.

Yoon, K. S., Duncan, T., Lee, S. W.-Y., Scarloss, B., & Shapley, K. (2007). Reviewing the evidence on how teacher professional development affects student achievement (Issues & Answers Report, REL 2007–No. 033). Available at http://ies.ed.gov/ncee/edlabs/regions/southwest/pdf/REL_2007033.pdf

Yuan, K., & Le, V. (2012). *Estimating the percentage of students who were tested on cognitively demanding items through the state achievement tests* (WR-967-WFHF). Santa Monica, CA: RAND Corporation.

Index

Note: The letter "n" refers to the reference note number on the page for the author citation.